India's
Undernourished
Children

7

Health, Nutrition, and Population Series

India's Undernourished Children

A Call for Reform and Action

Michele Gragnolati
Caryn Bredenkamp
Meera Shekar
Monica Das Gupta
Yi-Kyoung Lee

THE WORLD BANK
Washington, DC

ISBN-10: 0-8213-6587-8   eISBN: 0-8213-6588-6
ISBN-13: 978-0-8213-6587-8   DOI: 10.1596/978-0-8213-6587-8

Library of Congress Cataloging-in-Publication Data *has been applied for.*

Contents

Figures, Tables, and Boxes

Figures

viii • Figures, Tables, and Boxes

Tables

Boxes

Foreword

India has one of the highest rates of malnutrition in the world. Nearly one in every two of India's 120 million children is underweight, almost double the prevalence in Sub-Saharan Africa. An undernourished child will fail to reach her human potential in her adult years—in terms of educational attainment, health and productivity—perpetuating a vicious cycle of poverty and malnutrition.

Progress in reducing the number of undernourished children in India over the past decade has been slower than in comparable countries. The shockingly high levels of undernutrition are exacerbated by significant and increasing inequalities across states and socioeconomic groups—girls, rural areas, the poorest, and scheduled tribes and castes are the worst affected.

Halving the prevalence of underweight children by 2015 is a key indicator of progress towards the Millennium Development Goal (MDG) of eradicating extreme poverty and hunger. Achieving the target will require difficult choices. It cannot be met by economic growth alone, however impressive that may be at the present time.

In India, until recently, food insecurity has been viewed as the primary or even sole cause of child malnutrition. By contrast, research indicates that high levels of exposure to infection and inappropriate child feeding and caring practices, especially during the first two to three years of life, are salient. This misperception has resulted in resources being skewed towards ineffective food-based interventions.

India's main early child development intervention, the Integrated Child Development Services program (ICDS), has been operating for about 30 years. While it has certainly had some successes, it does not appear to have made a significant dent in child malnutrition. There are two main reasons. First, it has prioritized food supplementation over nutrition and health education interventions. Second, it has focused on children above the age of three, by which time the irreversible effects of malnutrition have already set in. Transforming the ICDS into an intervention that effectively addresses the principal causes of malnutrition will yield huge human and economic benefits for India. However, this will require substantial changes in the program's design and implementation. In particular, public investments in the ICDS should be redirected towards the younger children (0–3 years) and the most vulnerable population groups within those states and districts with a high prevalence of undernutrition. The focus should be on those ICDS components that directly address the most important causes of undernutrition in India, specifically improving child feeding and care behaviors, strengthening the referral to the health system, and providing micronutrients.

The Government of India recently launched the National Rural Health Mission and the National Nutrition Mission, and has also committed itself to rapidly expand the ICDS program. A review of the characteristics of undernutrition in India and of the ICDS is therefore particularly timely. This report analyzes the successes and failures of current child nutrition policy in India and identifies effective policies and programs which could significantly reduce the current high levels of child malnutrition, and, in so doing, help break the cycle of malnutrition and poverty.

Julian Schweitzer
Director
Human Development Department
South Asia Region

Prafu Patel
Vice President
South Asia Region

Acknowledgments

Work on this report has been supported by generous funding from the Netherlands Ministry of Foreign Affairs, through the Bank-Netherlands Partnership Program.

The report was authored by Michele Gragnolati (task team leader), Caryn Bredenkamp (University of North Carolina at Chapel Hill), Meera Shekar, Monica Das Gupta (World Bank), and Yi-Kyoung Lee (World Bank). A number of background papers were prepared in advance of the first draft. These include:

"Who Does India's ICDS Nutrition Program Reach, and What Effect Does It Have?" by Monica Das Gupta, Michael Lokshin, and Oleksiy Ivaschenko (Development Economics Research Group [DECRG], World Bank).

"Case Study on Mid-Day Meal Scheme of Tamil Nadu and Gujarat," by P. Subramaniyam.

"Analysis of Public Expenditures and Impact of Public Distribution System (PDS) on Food Security," by S. Mahendra Dev.

"India's Integrated Child Development Services Scheme: Meeting the Health and Nutritional Needs of Children, Adolescent Girls and Women?" by Caryn Bredenkamp and John S. Akin (University of North Carolina at Chapel Hill).

"Literature Review of MDM, ICDS, and PDS (1992–2003), Including Annotated Bibliography," by New Concept Information Systems, India.

"Analysis of Positive Deviance in the ICDS Program in Rajasthan and Uttar Pradesh," by Educational Resource Unit, India.

"Monitoring and Evaluation in India's ICDS Programme," by Saroj K. Adhikari, Department of Women and Child Development, Government of India.

"Reviewing the Costs of Malnutrition in India," by Laveesh Bhandari and Lehar Zaidi, Indicus Analytics, India.

"Will Asia Meet the Nutrition Millennium Development Goal? and Even If It Does, Will It Be Enough?" by Meera Shekar (HDNHE, World Bank), Mercedes de Onis, Monika Blössner, and Elaine Borghi (Department of Nutrition for Health and Development, World Health Organization).

Peer reviewers were Prof. Abhijit Sen (Planning Commission, Government of India), Ruth Levine (Center for Global Development), and Harold Alderman (DECRG, World Bank). The final report was strengthened by valuable comments from the Department of Women and Child Development (DWCD), Government of India.

A number of technical experts provided inputs and reviews at various stages of the report's development. Peer reviewers involved in the conceptualization of the project were Ruth Levine (Center for Global Development), John S. Akin (University of North Carolina at Chapel Hill), Harold Alderman, Meera Shekar, and Jishnu Das (World Bank). Additional analysis of various data underpinning the report was performed by Peter Heywood, Himani Pruthi, Jayshree Balachander, Venkatachalam Selvaraju and Julie Babinard (World Bank and consultants to the World Bank). Information on some of the case studies included in this report was generously shared by Deepika Chaudhery, T. Usha Kiran, and others at CARE-India. Additional inputs and comments were received from Paoli Belli, Alan Berg, Barbara Kafka (World Bank), Werner Schultnik (UNICEF, India), and Arun Gupta.

The Government of India and respective State Governments provided data from a baseline survey of the ICDS III program and an endline survey of the ICDS II program. These data were collected by research teams at six research organizations, namely Agricultural Finance Corporation (AFCIndia), Indian Institute of Development

Management (IIDM), Indian Institute of Health Management Research (IIHMR), ORG Centre for Social Research, Rajagiri College of Sciences (RCSS), and Xavier Institute of Social Sciences (XISS).

Overall project guidance and specific comments were provided by Anabela Abreu, Peter Berman, Charlie Griffin, Meera Priyadarshi, and Julian Schweitzer. Program support and administrative assistance were provided by Nira Singh and Elfreda Vincent, and editorial and publishing assistance by Rama Lakshminarayanan, Miyuki Parris, Jennifer Vito, Paola Scalabrin, and Mark Ingebretsen.

Abbreviations

ANC	antenatal care
ANM	auxiliary nurse-midwife
AWC	*anganwadi* center
AWH	*anganwadi* helper
AWW	*anganwadi* worker
BMI	body mass index
CDPO	Child Development Project Officer
DALY	disability-adjusted life year
DHFW	Department of Health and Family Welfare
DHS	Demographic and Health Survey
DWCD	Department of Women and Child Development
GDP	gross domestic product
HAZ	height-for-age z-score
ICDS	Integrated Child Development Services
ICN	International Conference on Nutrition
IDA	iron deficiency anemia
IDD	iodine deficiency disorder
IFA	iron and folic acid
IMR	infant mortality rate
LAC	Latin America and the Caribbean
LHW	lady health-worker
M&E	monitoring and evaluation
MDG	Millennium Development Goal
MoHFW	Ministry of Health and Family Welfare
NFHS	National Family Health Survey
NID	National Immunization Day
PEM	protein energy malnutrition

PPP	purchasing power parity
PRI	*panchayat raj* institution
RCH	reproductive and child health program
SAR	South Asia Region
SNP	supplementary nutrition program
TB	tuberculosis
VAD	Vitamin A deficiency
VPD	vaccine preventable disease
WAZ	weight-for-age z-score
WCD	women and child development
WHZ	weight-for-height z-score

Overview

The World Bank has supported efforts to improve nutrition in India since 1980, with mixed results. This report aims at helping policymakers by providing information on the characteristics of child malnutrition in India and on the effectiveness of the Integrated Child Development Services (ICDS) program in addressing the causes and symptoms of undernutrition. The report identifies the most important mismatches between the program's intentions and its implementation and presents some options for resolving the mismatches and creating a more effective, efficient, and equitable program.

A short summary of each of the three chapters of the report is presented below.

Chapter 1: Dimensions of Child Undernutrition in India

Child undernutrition has enormous consequences for child and adult morbidity and mortality. In addition, undernutrition reduces productivity, so that a failure to invest in combating malnutrition effectively diminishes the potential for economic growth.

In India, the situation is dire: the prevalence of underweight among children is nearly twice that of Sub-Saharan Africa, and inequalities in undernutrition between demographic, socioeconomic, and geographic groups have been increasing. More, and better, investments are needed if India is to reach the nutrition Millennium Development Goal (MDG) target. Economic growth alone will not be enough.

Undernutrition—both protein-energy malnutrition and micronutrient deficiencies—directly affects many aspects of children's development. It retards their physical and cognitive growth and increases susceptibility to infection and disease, further increasing the probability of being malnourished. As a result, undernutrition has been estimated to be associated with about half of all child deaths. More than half of child deaths from diarrhea (61 percent), malaria (57 percent), and pneumonia (52 percent) are associated with malnutrition, as well as 45 percent of deaths from measles. Child undernutrition in India is responsible for 22 percent of the country's burden of disease.

Undernutrition also affects cognitive and motor development, and it undermines educational attainment. Ultimately, it affects productivity at work and at home, with adverse implications for income and economic growth. Micronutrient deficiencies alone may be costing India $2.5 billion a year.

Most growth retardation occurs by the age of 2—in part because about 30 percent of Indian children are born with low birth weight—and it is largely irreversible. In 1998/99 (the latest year for which nationally representative data are available), almost three-quarters of Indian children under age 3 were below the normal weight for their age, with 47 percent underweight or severely underweight and another 26 percent mildly underweight.

Levels of malnutrition declined modestly in the 1990s, with the prevalence of underweight among children under 3 falling 11 percent between 1992/93 and 1998/99. This progress lags far behind that achieved by countries with similar economic growth rates.

Disaggregation of underweight statistics by socioeconomic and demographic characteristics reveals which groups are at greatest risk of malnutrition. Underweight prevalence is higher in rural areas (50 percent) than in urban areas (38 percent), higher among girls (49 percent) than among boys (46 percent), higher among scheduled castes (53 percent) and scheduled tribes (56 percent) than among other castes (44 percent), and although it is pervasive throughout the wealth distribution, the prevalence of underweight reaches as high as 60 percent in the lowest wealth quintile. Moreover, during the 1990s, urban-rural, intercaste, male-female, and interquintile inequalities in nutritional status widened.

Interstate variation in the patterns and trends in underweight is large. In six states (Bihar, Madhya Pradesh, Maharashtra, Orissa, Rajasthan, and Uttar Pradesh), at least half of all children are underweight. Four states—Bihar, Madhya Pradesh, Rajasthan, and Uttar Pradesh—account for more than 43 percent of all underweight children in India.

Moreover, the prevalence of underweight is falling more slowly in high-prevalence states.

The demographic and socioeconomic patterns at the state level do not necessarily mirror those at the national level. In some states, for example, inequalities in underweight are narrowing, not widening; in others, boys are more likely to be underweight than girls. Nutrition policy should take these differences into account.

Undernutrition is concentrated in a relatively small number of districts and villages, with a mere 10 percent of villages and districts accounting for 27–28 percent of all underweight children and a quarter of districts and villages accounting for more than half of all underweight children. This distribution suggests that future efforts to combat malnutrition could give priority to a relatively small number of districts and villages.

Micronutrient deficiencies are also widespread in India. More than 75 percent of preschool children suffer from iron deficiency anemia, and 57 percent have subclinical Vitamin A deficiency. Iodine deficiency is endemic in 85 percent of districts. Progress in reducing the prevalence of micronutrient deficiencies in India has been modest. As with underweight, the prevalence of different micronutrient deficiencies varies widely across states.

Economic growth alone is unlikely to be sufficient to significantly lower the prevalence of malnutrition—it will certainly not be sufficient to meet the MDG target of halving the prevalence of underweight children between 1990 and 2015. Only by rapidly scaling up health, nutrition, education, and infrastructure interventions and improving their effectiveness can this target be met. This is especially critical in the poorest states.

Chapter 2: The Integrated Child Development Services Program (ICDS)

India's primary policy response to child malnutrition, the ICDS program, is well conceived and well placed to address the major causes of child undernutrition in India. But more attention has been given to increasing coverage than to improving the quality of service delivery, and the program has focused more on distributing food than on changing family-based feeding and caring behavior. As a result, impact has been limited.

The ICDS has expanded tremendously over its 30 years of operation to cover almost all development blocks in India. It offers a wide range of health, nutrition, and education services to children, women, and adolescent girls. The program is intended to target the needs of the poorest and the most undernourished, as well as the age groups that represent a "window of opportunity" for nutrition investments (that is, children under 3 and pregnant and lactating women). There is a mismatch, however, between the program's intentions and its actual implementation:

- The central focus on food supplementation drains resources from other tasks envisaged in the program that are crucial for improving child nutritional outcomes. For example, not enough attention is given to educating parents about how to improve childcare behaviors and feeding practices.

- Older children (3–6) participate much more than younger ones, and many children from poorer households do not yet participate. The program fails to preferentially target girls, children from lower castes, or children from the poorest villages, all of whom are at higher risk of undernutrition.

- Although expansion of the program was greater in underserved than well-served areas during the 1990s, the poorest states and those with the highest levels of undernutrition still have the lowest levels of program funding and coverage by ICDS activities.

In addition to these mismatches, the program faces substantial operational challenges. Inadequate worker skills, shortages of equipment, poor supervision, and weak monitoring and evaluation reduce the program's potential impact. Community workers are overburdened, because they are expected to provide preschool education to 4- to 6-year-olds as well as nutrition services to all children under 6. As a result, most children under 3—for whom nutrition interventions can have the largest impact—do not receive micronutrient supplements, and most of their parents are not reached with counseling on better feeding and childcare practices. Examples of successful ICDS interventions (in some districts) and innovations and variants of ICDS in several states (the INHP II in nine states, the Dular scheme in Bihar, and the Tamil Nadu

Integrated Nutrition Project) suggest that the potential for better implementation and greater impact does exist.

Chapter 3: Enhancing the Impact of ICDS

ICDS was designed to address the multidimensional causes of malnutrition. As the program expands to reach more and more villages, it has tremendous potential to improve the well-being of the millions of women and children who are eligible for participation. The key constraint on its effectiveness is that implementation deviates from the original design.

Realizing ICDS' potential will require substantial commitment and resources in order to realign its implementation with its original objectives and design. Several steps need to be taken:

- Ambiguity over the priority of different program objectives and interventions must be resolved.

- Activities need to be refocused on the most important determinants of malnutrition. Programmatically, this means emphasizing disease control and prevention activities, education to improve domestic childcare and feeding practices, and micronutrient supplementation. Greater convergence with the health sector, in particular the Reproductive and Child Health Program, would help tremendously in this regard.

- Activities need to better target the most vulnerable age groups (children under 3 and pregnant women). Funds and new projects need to be redirected to the states and districts with the highest prevalence of malnutrition.

- Supplementary feeding activities need to better target those who need them most, and growth-monitoring activities need to be performed with greater regularity, with an emphasis on using this process to help parents understand how to improve their children's health and nutrition.

- Communities need to be involved in implementing and monitoring ICDS, in order to bring additional resources to the *anganwadi* centers, improve the quality of service delivery, and increase accountability in the system.

• Monitoring and evaluation activities need to be strengthened through the collection of timely, relevant, accessible, high-quality information, and this information needs to be used to improve program functioning by shifting the focus from inputs to results, using data to inform decisions, and creating accountability for performance.

CHAPTER 1

Dimensions of Child Undernutrition in India

Child undernutrition has enormous consequences for morbidity and mortality. It also affects productivity, so that failure to invest in nutrition today reduces potential economic growth tomorrow. In India, where the prevalence of undernutrition is nearly twice that of Sub-Saharan Africa, the situation is dire. More, and better, investments are needed if undernutrition is to be reduced; growing inequalities in nutrition across demographic, socioeconomic, and geographic groups diminished; and the nutrition Millennium Development Goal (MDG) target reached. Economic growth alone will not be enough.

The prevalence of underweight among children in India is among the highest in the world (box 1.1). About 37 million children under the age of 3 are underweight, and many more suffer from various micronutrient deficiencies. In recent years, the prevalence of undernutrition has declined only slightly. Dealing with malnutrition is thus an urgent policy priority (World Bank 2004a).[1]

As a result of undernutrition, the distribution of children's age-standardized weight is far to the left of the global reference standard (figure 1.1). In 1998/99 (the latest year for which nationally representative data are available), almost three-quarters of Indian children under 3 were below the normal weight for their age. Forty-seven percent were underweight, of which 18 percent were severely underweight and 26 percent were mildly underweight. About 46 percent of children were stunted, and 16 percent could be classified as wasted. Given that even mild malnutrition is linked to a twofold increase in

Box 1.1 How is malnutrition defined?

Nutritional status is typically described in terms of anthropometric indices, such as underweight, stunting, and wasting. These terms are measures of protein-energy undernutrition and are used to describe children who have a weight-for-age, height- (or recumbent length-) for-age, and weight-for-height that is less than two standard deviations below the median value of the National Center for Health Statistics–World Health Organization (WHO) reference group. These children are considered to suffer from moderate malnutrition. The terms *severe underweight, severe stunting,* and *severe wasting* are used when the measurements are less than three standard deviations below the reference median; *mild underweight, stunting,* and *wasting* refer to measurements of less than one standard deviation below the reference population. *Underweight* is generally considered a composite measure of long- and short-term nutritional status; *stunting* reflects long-term nutritional status, and *wasting* is an indicator of acute short-term undernutrition. Some indicators of micronutrient malnutrition are also used to measure malnutrition. The most commons forms of micronutrient malnutrition referred to in this report are Vitamin A deficiency, iodine deficiency disorders, and iron-deficiency anemia.

mortality and to greatly reduced productivity levels, these levels of undernutrition significantly compromise health and productivity.

The nutritional status of children improved modestly during the 1990s. Between 1992/93 and 1998/99, the prevalence of underweight fell almost 11 percent, equivalent to a 1.5 percent annual reduction (figure 1.2). But this improvement lagged far behind that achieved by countries with similar economic growth rates.

Figure 1.1 The weight-for-age distribution for children under 3 in India compares unfavorably with the global distribution

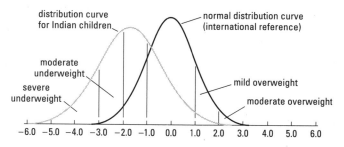

Source: Calculated from NFHS II (1998/99) data.

Figure 1.2 The prevalence of undernutrition in children under 3 fell modestly in India, 1992 and 1998

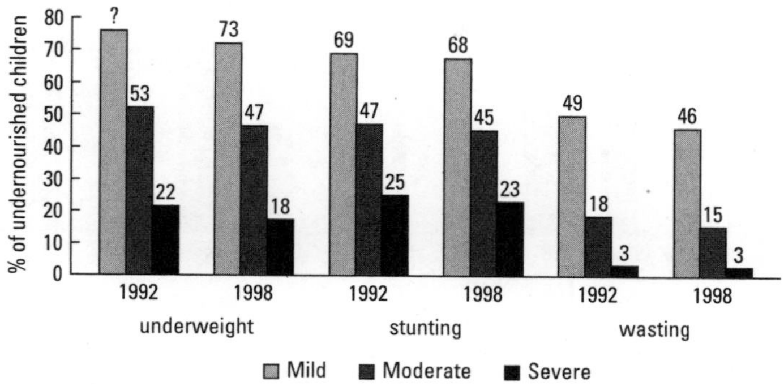

Source: NFHS I (1992/93) and NFHS II (1998/99).

The reduction was in line with gains made earlier (figure 1.3). According to the WHO Global Database on Child Growth and Nutrition (WHO 2004c), the prevalence of malnutrition among children under 5 in rural India fell from more than 70 percent in the late 1970s to less than 50 percent at the end of the 1990s for both underweight and stunting measures. The prevalence of severe stunting also declined over this period, from almost 50 percent to less than 25 percent, while the prevalence of severe underweight declined from 37 percent to less than 20 percent.

The prevalence of micronutrient deficiencies among children and women of reproductive age in India is consistently among the highest in the world (table 1.1). More than 75 percent of preschool children suffer from iron deficiency anemia. Up to 60 percent have subclinical Vitamin A deficiency, although less than 2 percent suffer from clinical Vitamin A deficiency.[2] About one in four school children has goiter, a sign of severe iodine deficiency (UNICEF 2003b; WHO 2000; UNICEF and MI 2004a). Among ever-married women 15–49, 52 percent have some degree of anemia, with the prevalence of anemia among some groups of pregnant women reaching 87 percent. Clinical Vitamin A deficiency affects about 5 percent of women and subclinical Vitamin A deficiency about 12 percent of women. Iodine deficiency in pregnant women in India is estimated to have caused the congenital mental impairment of about 6.6 million children (IIPS and Orc Macro 2000; UNICEF 2003b).

Figure 1.3 The prevalence of underweight and stunting among children under 5 in rural India fell between the mid-1970s and the late 1990s

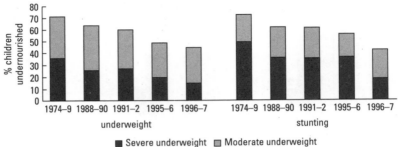

Severe underweight ■ Moderate underweight ■

Source: WHO 2004a.
Note: Prevalence is not strictly comparable across time periods, since each round of surveys used different sampling methodologies and calculated prevalence across different age groups.

Why Invest in Combating Undernutrition?

Failing to deal effectively with the undernutrition problem in India has dire consequences for children's development. It retards their physical growth and increases their susceptibility to disease in childhood and adulthood. It also affects cognitive and motor development, limits educational attainment and productivity, and ultimately perpetuates poverty. Moreover, in a country where undernutrition is so widespread, the consequences of undernutrition go well beyond the individual, affecting total labor-force productivity and economic growth.

Effect of Undernutrition on Morbidity, Mortality, and Cognitive and Motor Development

By precipitating disease and speeding its progression, malnutrition is a leading contributor to infant, child, and maternal mortality and morbidity. It has been estimated to play a role in about half of all child deaths (Horton 1999; Pelletier and others 1995; Pelletier and Frongillo 2003), and in more than half of child deaths from diarrhea (61 percent), malaria (57 percent), and pneumonia (52 percent). Malnutrition is also involved in 45 percent of all child deaths from measles (Black, Morris, and Bryce 2003; Caulfield and others 2004). Pediatric malnutrition is a risk factor for 16 percent of the global burden of dis-

Table 1.1 Prevalence of micronutrient deficiencies in selected countries in South Asia (percent except where indicated otherwise)

Country	Iron deficiency anemia				Vitamin A deficiency			Iodine deficiency			Folate deficiency
	In children under 5	In women 15-49	In pregnant women	Number of maternal deaths from severe anemia per year	Children under 6 with subclinical Vitamin A deficiency	Children under 6 with clinical Vitamin A deficiency	Number of child deaths precipitated	Total goiter rate among school children	Total goiter rate	Number of children born mentally impaired per year	Number of neural tube defects per year
Afghanistan	65	61	—	—	—	53	50,000	—	48	535,000	2,250
Bangladesh	55	36	74	2,800	0.7	28	28,000	50	18	750,000	8,400
Bhutan	81	55	68	<100	0.7	32	600	14	—	—	150
India	75	51	87	22,000	0.7	57	330,000	19	26	6,600,000	50,000
Nepal	65	62	63	760	1.0	33	6,900	40	24	200,000	1,600
Pakistan	56	59	—	—	—	35	56,000	—	38	2,100,000	11,000
South Asia region	—	—	—	25,560	—	—	471,500	—	—	10,185,000	73,400
World	—	—	—	50,000	—	—	1,150,000	—	—	19,000,000	204,000

Source: UNICEF 2003b; WHO 2000; UNICEF and MI 2004a.

— Not available.

ease, but it accounts for as much as 22 percent of India's burden of disease (Murray and Lopez 1997).

Consequences of Protein-Energy Malnutrition Isolating the effects of protein and energy deficiencies on health and development outcomes is confounded by the fact that when food intake is low, the intake of many other nutrients is usually also inadequate (Allen 1994).[3] Nevertheless, it is generally accepted that children who are underweight or stunted are at greater risk for childhood morbidity and mortality, poor physical and mental development, inferior school performance, and reduced adult size and capacity for work (WHO 1995).

Protein-energy malnutrition weakens immune response and exacerbates the effects of infection (Pelletier and Frongillo 2003). As a result, children who are malnourished tend to have more severe diarrheal episodes and are at a higher risk of pneumonia. Infections, in turn, contribute to malnutrition, through a variety of mechanisms, including loss of appetite and reduced capacity to absorb nutrients (Calder and Jackson 2000).

Underweight and stunted women are also at higher risk of obstetric complications (because of smaller pelvic size) and low birth weight deliveries (ACC/SCN 1997). The result is an intergenerational cycle of malnutrition, since low birth weight infants tend to attain smaller stature as adults.

Malnutrition in early infancy is also correlated with increased susceptibility to chronic disease in adulthood, including coronary heart disease, diabetes, and high blood pressure (Agarwal and others 1998; Agarwal and others 2002; Barker and others 2001; Lucas, Fewtrell, and Cole 1999; Popkin and others 2001; UNICEF 1998).

Although the precise mechanisms are not clear, protein-energy malnutrition during the last trimester of pregnancy and the first two years of life is also associated with poor cognitive and motor development. The magnitude of the effect depends on the severity and duration of malnutrition as well as its timing: moderate protein-energy malnutrition of long-term duration has worse consequences for cognitive development than transient severe undernutrition.

Consequences of Micronutrient Deficiencies Iron and Vitamin A deficiencies are leading risk factors for disease in developing countries, especially countries with high mortality rates (WHO 2002). Iodine deficiency also carries a mortality risk.

Vitamin A deficiency. Vitamin A deficiency is a well-known cause of morbidity and mortality, especially among young children and pregnant women. In young children, clinical Vitamin A deficiency can cause xerophthalmia (a dry, thickened, lusterless condition of the eyeball) and keratomalacia (a softening, drying, and ulceration of the cornea), and it can lead to blindness (Vinutha, Metha, and Shanbag 2000). Subclinical Vitamin A deficiency, defined by a serum retinol concentration of less than 0.7 μmol/L, can limit children's growth, weaken the immune system, exacerbate infection, and increase the risk of death (West 2002), mainly from respiratory and gastrointestinal infections. Often occurring concurrently among children with protein-energy malnutrition, Vitamin A deficiency is estimated to be responsible for about 1 million child deaths a year (Mason and others 2005). Pregnant women, especially in the third trimester, when micronutrient demands are at their highest, often exhibit a high prevalence of night blindness. Recent studies have shown that Vitamin A deficiency may also be associated with an increased risk of mother-to-child transmission of HIV, although Vitamin A supplementation fails to lower the risk of transmission (Stephenson 2003). In general, Vitamin A supplementation has proven successful in reducing the incidence and severity of illness, and it has been associated with a reduction in child mortality of 25–35 percent (Beaton, Martorell, and Aronson 1993; Fawzi, Chalmers, and Herrera 1993), especially from diarrhea, measles, and malaria (Jones and others 2003).

Iron deficiency anemia. Iron deficiency anemia is common across all age groups, although its incidence is highest among children and pregnant and lactating women. It affects about 2 billion people in developing countries. The consequences of iron deficiency anemia in pregnant women include increased risk of low birth weight or premature delivery, perinatal and neonatal mortality, inadequate iron stores for the newborn, lowered physical activity, fatigue, and increased risk of maternal morbidity (Bentley and Griffiths 2003). It is also responsible for almost a quarter of maternal deaths (Ross and Thomas 1996). Inadequate iron stores in a newborn child, coupled with insufficient iron intake during the weaning period, have been shown to impair intellectual development by adversely affecting language, cognitive, and motor development. Iron deficiency among adults contributes to low labor productivity (WHO 2004c; Seshadri 2001).

Iodine deficiency. Iodine deficiency during pregnancy is associated with low birth weight, increased likelihood of stillbirth, spontaneous abortion, and congenital abnormalities such as cretinism and irreversible forms of mental impairment. During childhood it impairs physical growth, causes goiter, and decreases the probability of child survival. It is also the most common cause of preventable mental retardation and brain damage in the world (ACC/SCN 2000). Globally, 2.2 billion people (38 percent of the world's population) live in regions where iodine deficiency is endemic (WHO 2002).

Both iodine and iron deficiencies have been linked to the retardation of cognitive processes in infants and young children. Maternal iodine deficiency has negative and irreversible effects on the cognitive functioning of the developing fetus. Postnatal iodine deficiency may also be associated with cognitive deficits (Black 2003): IQs of iodine-deficient children have been shown to average 13.5 points less than iodine-sufficient children (Bleichrodt and Born 1994); iron deficiency anemia has been associated with half a standard deviation reduction in IQ (Ross and Horton 1998).

Effect of Undernutrition on Schooling, Adult Productivity, and Economic Growth

The cognitive and physical consequences of undernutrition—both underweight and micronutrient deficiencies—undermine educational attainment and labor productivity, with adverse implications for income and economic growth. Malnutrition at any stage of childhood affects schooling and thus lifetime earnings potential (Alderman 2005). Some of the pathways through which malnutrition affects educational outcomes include the reduced capacity to learn (as a result of early cognitive deficits or lowered current attention span) and the reduction in the number of total years of schooling (since caregivers may invest less in malnourished children or schools may use child size as an indicator of school readiness) (Alderman 2005). In rural Pakistan, malnutrition has been found to decrease the probability of ever attending school, particularly for girls (Alderman and others 2001). In the Philippines, children with higher nutritional status during the preschool years start primary school earlier; repeat fewer grades (Glewwe, Jacoby, and King 2001); and have higher high school completion rates (Daniels and Adair 2004) than other children. In Zimbabwe, stunting, through its association with a seven-month delay in school completion and a 0.7-year loss in grade attainment, has been shown to reduce lifetime income by 7–12 percent (Alderman, Hentschel, and Sabates 2003).

Measuring the productivity losses associated with undernutrition is complex, and since different studies incorporate different types of productivity gains, estimates can vary widely.[4] Moreover, since a large share of productivity losses are measured in terms of forgone wages, when productivity losses are expressed in dollar terms rather than as a percentage of GDP, the productivity losses in India may appear small relative to countries with higher average wages. In general, in low-income agricultural countries in Asia, the physical impairment associated with malnutrition is estimated to cost more than 2–3 percent of GDP a year—even without considering the long-term productivity losses associated with developmental and cognitive impairment (Horton 1999). Iron deficiency in adults has been estimated to decrease productivity by 5–17 percent, depending on the nature of the work performed (Horton 1999). Data from 10 developing countries show that the median loss in reduced work capacity associated with anemia during adulthood is equivalent to 0.6 percent of GDP, while an additional 3.4 percent of GDP is lost due to the effects on cognitive development attributable to anemia during childhood (Horton and Ross 2003). The impact of iodine deficiency disorders on cognitive development alone has been associated with productivity losses of about 10 percent of GDP (Horton 1999).

A few attempts have been made to estimate the productivity losses associated with malnutrition in India. As with global estimates, these estimates are intrinsically imprecise, requiring many assumptions and approximations. One study projects that in the absence of appropriate interventions, the productivity losses due to protein-energy malnutrition, iodine deficiency disorder, and iron deficiency anemia are likely to equal about $114 billion between 2003 and 2012 (Care India and Linkages India 2003). Another study, examining only the productivity losses associated with forgone wage employment resulting from child malnutrition, estimates the loss at $2.3 billion a year (Bhandari and Zaidi 2004). Other studies suggest that micronutrient deficiencies alone may cost India $2.5 billion a year (Alderman 2005) and that stunting, iodine deficiency, and iron deficiency together are responsible for a total productivity loss of almost 3 percent of GDP among manual workers alone (Horton 1999) (table 1.2).

Table 1.2   Estimated productivity losses due to malnutrition in India

Item	Disability-adjusted life years lost due to malnutrition in India	Estimated total annual losses due to malnutrition (billions of dollars)	Estimated loss of adult productivity (percent of GDP)
Protein-energy malnutrition (stunting)	2,939,000	8.1	1.4
Vitamin A deficiency	404,000	0.4	—
Iodine deficiency disorder	214,000	1.5	0.3
Iron deficiency	3,672,000	6.3	1.25

Source: ASC 1998; World Bank 2004c; Horton 1999.
— Not available.
Note: Productivity losses include market activities only.

Prevalence of Underweight

An International Perspective

Undernutrition in India is among the worst in the world (table 1.3). In the late 1990s, the prevalence of underweight (47 percent) was about the same as in Bangladesh and Nepal (48 percent), but it was much higher than in all other countries in South Asia. It was also far higher than the averages for other regions of the world and nearly double that of Sub-Saharan Africa (box 1.2). High prevalence combined with

Table 1.3   Percentage of children suffering from underweight, stunting, and wasting, by world region and country, 2000

Region/country	Underweight	Stunting	Wasting
Latin America and Caribbean	6	14	2
Africa	24	35	8
Asia	28	30	9
India	47	45	16
Bangladesh	48	45	10
Bhutan	19	40	3
Maldives	45	36	20
Nepal	48	51	10
Pakistan	40	36	14
Sri Lanka	33	20	13
All developing countries	22–27	28–32	7–9

Source: ACC/SCN 2004.

India's large population means that of the 150 million malnourished children under the age of 5 in the world, more than a third live in India (UNICEF 2003b; ACC/SCN 2000; DWCD 2003).

The decline in the prevalence of underweight during the 1990s was less rapid than in most other countries with similar socioeconomic or geographical characteristics (figure 1.4). Although per capita GDP in India rose by an average annual rate of 5.3 percent, the average annual prevalence of underweight fell just 1.5 percent a year. In some other countries, underweight prevalence fell more than 5 percent, even though annual per capita GDP growth was 2 percent or less. In China, where annual growth averaged 12 percent, the prevalence of child

---

Box 1.2   The "South Asian enigma": Why is undernutrition so much higher in South Asia than in Sub-Saharan Africa?

In 1997, when Ramalingaswami, Jonson, and Rohde wrote that "in the public imagi-nation, the home of the malnourished child is Sub-Saharan Africa ... but ... the worst affected region is not Africa but South Asia," their statement was met with incredulity. Today, undernutrition rates in South Asia, including and especially in India, are nearly twice those in Sub-Saharan Africa. This is not an artifact of different measurement standards or differing growth potential among ethnic groups: studies have repeatedly shown that given similar opportunities, children across most ethnic groups, including Indian children, can grow to the same levels and that the same internationally recognized growth references can be used across countries to assess the prevalence of malnutrition (Nutrition Foundation of India 1991). The phe-nomenon referred to as the "South Asian enigma" is real.

The enigma can be explained by three key differences between South Asia and Sub-Saharan Africa:

More than 30 percent of Indian babies are born with low birth weights, compared with about 16 percent in Sub-Saharan Africa. Low birth weight is the single most important predictor of undernutrition.

Women in South Asia tend to have lower status and less decision-making power than women in Sub-Saharan Africa, limiting their ability to access the resources needed for their own and their children's health and nutrition. Low status of women can be linked to low birth weight, as well as poor child-feeding behaviors in the first 12 months of life.

Hygiene and sanitation standards in South Asia are well below those in Sub-Saha-ran Africa. Poor hygiene and sanitation play a major role in causing the infections that lead to undernutrition in the first two years of life.

Figure 1.4 In terms of underweight, India compares poorly with other countries at similar levels of economic development

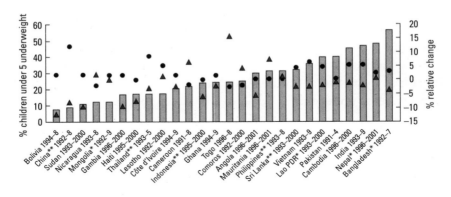

□ Prevalence (left axis)
▲ Annual change, prevalence underweight children (right axis)
● Annual change, GDP per capita, purchasing power parity (right axis)

Source: World Bank 2004b, e.
Note: Countries in Asia with per capita GDP of less than $1,333 are denoted by *; countries in Asia with per capita GDP of more than $2,333 are denoted by **. Purchasing power parity is in constant 1995 international dollars.
Criteria for inclusion in the graph were as follows: At least two household surveys were conducted between 1990 and 2002 in each of the countries displayed. When more than two surveys were available, information collected around 1992/93 and 1998/99 was used, to enhance comparability with data from India's NFHS. Countries with a prevalence of underweight among children under 5 of less than 10 percent in the first survey were dropped. Countries are either in Asia or are comparable to India in terms of per capita GDP at purchasing power parity (1995 constant international dollars), that is, have per capita GDP of $1,333–$2,333 (India's per capita GDP was $1,833 in 1995).

underweight fell at an annual rate of more than 8 percent. In Bangladesh, despite economic growth that lagged behind that of India, the decline in the prevalence of underweight was greater (3.5 percent).

Patterns and Trends in India

The prevalence of underweight among children under 3 and recent trends in underweight vary substantially across demographic and socioeconomic groups in India (table 1.4). In 1998/99, the prevalence of underweight was much higher in rural areas (50 percent) than in urban areas (38 percent), and the differences were even larger for severe underweight, which affected 20 percent of rural children and 12 percent of urban children.

Table 1.4 Prevalence of underweight and severe underweight in children under 3, by demographic and socioeconomic group, 1992/93–1998/99

Item	Underweight			Severe underweight		
	Prevalence 1992/93	Prevalence 1998/99	Percentage change	Prevalence 1992/93	Prevalence 1998/99	Percentage change
Total	53	47	−11	22	18	−18
Urban	44	38	−13	16	12	−27
Rural	55	50	−10	24	20	−16
Quintile 1 (poorest)	61	59	−4	30	27	−8
Quintile 2	60	56	−6	26	23	−12
Quintile 3	56	52	−6	23	21	−7
Quintile 4	49	44	−11	18	15	−12
Quintile 5 (richest)	36	33	−9	11	9	−26
Female	52	49	−6	21	19	−11
Male	53	46	−15	22	17	−24
Scheduled castes	57	53	−7	25	21	−15
Scheduled tribes	57	56	−2	29	26	−9
Other castes	51	44	−14	20	16	−23

Source: Calculated from NFHS I (1992/93) and NFHS II (1998/99) data.

Prevalence As expected, the prevalence of both underweight and severe underweight increases as household wealth falls, although at a decreasing rate. Underweight prevalence was as high as 60 percent in the lowest quintile, but it was so pervasive throughout the wealth distribution that even in the wealthiest fifth of the population 33 percent of children were underweight and 8 percent were severely underweight.

The prevalence of both underweight and severe underweight was slightly higher among girls than boys (49 percent versus 46 percent for underweight, 19 percent versus 17 percent for severe underweight). It was much higher among scheduled castes and scheduled tribes than among other castes.

Thus children at greatest risk for underweight are girls whose families are poor, belong to scheduled tribes or castes, and live in rural areas. Assuming independence of conditional probabilities, the chance that a girl with all these characteristics is underweight is as high as 92 percent (figure 1.5).[5]

Figure 1.5 Girls whose families are poor, belong to a scheduled tribe or caste, live in a rural area, and are at risk of being underweight

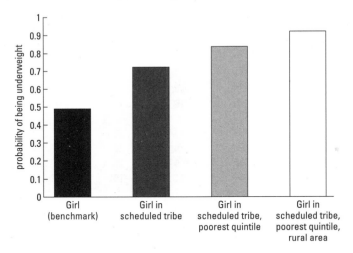

Source: Calculated from NFHS II (1998–9) data.

The age pattern of undernutrition is an important dimension of the problem in India—and indeed all over the world. Growth retardation occurs early in life, and most of this early damage is irreversible (ACC/SCN 2004). Most growth faltering occurs either during pregnancy (30 percent of children in India are born with low birth weight) or during the first two years of life.[6] Indeed, by the age of 2, most growth retardation has already taken place (figure 1.6). Consequently, the period between pregnancy and the first two years of life represents the "window of opportunity" in which to address undernutrition. Efforts to fight undernutrition need to focus on this age group.

Trends The prevalence of both underweight and severe underweight fell during the 1990s, but it fell less among segments of the population that were already more likely to be underweight in 1992/93. Consequently, over time, urban-rural, intercaste, male-female, and wealth inequalities in nutritional status widened (figure 1.7).

The percentage reduction in severe underweight prevalence between 1992–93 and 1998–99 was dramatically higher in urban areas (26 percent) than in rural areas (16 percent). The reduction was also somewhat greater for underweight prevalence.

Figure 1.6 By the age of 2, most of the damage from undernourishment has been done

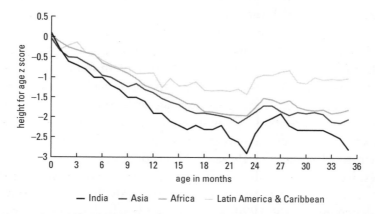

— India — Asia — Africa — Latin America & Caribbean

Source: Regional estimates from Shrimpton and others (2001); India data from IIPS and Orc
Macro (2000).
Note: For the pattern of age-specific weight-for-age estimates, see figure A.1 in the appendix.

Figure 1.7 Demographic and socioeconomic variation in prevalence of underweight
children under 3, 1992/93 to 1998/99

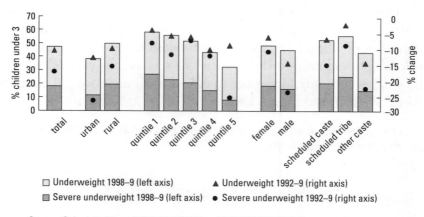

□ Underweight 1998–9 (left axis)   ▲ Underweight 1992–9 (right axis)
▨ Severe underweight 1998–9 (left axis)   ● Severe underweight 1992–9 (right axis)

Source: Calculated from NFHS I (1992/93) and NFHS II (1998/99) data.
Note: Quintile 1 is the poorest quintile, quintile 5 the richest.

By 1998/99 the percentage of underweight children in the bottom
two wealth quintiles had fallen below 60 percent. However, reductions in the percentage of malnourished children were lower in the
lower quintiles than in the upper quintiles, indicating the growing
health disparity between children of relatively low and relatively high

economic status. In fact, the greatest percentage reduction in the prevalence of underweight, especially severe underweight, accrued to children in the wealthiest quintiles.

Between 1992/93 and 1998/99, underweight prevalence among boys fell 14 percent (from 53 percent to 46 percent), while underweight prevalence among girls fell just 6 percent (from 52 percent to 49 percent). The effect was to reverse the underweight gender gap, so that, on aggregate in India, girls now lag far behind boys. The reversal was even more pronounced for severe underweight prevalence, which fell 24 percent (from 22 percent to 17 percent) for boys and 11 percent (from 21 percent to 19 percent) for girls.

Despite the ostensible targeting of nutrition and health interventions to vulnerable castes, the percentage decline in underweight prevalence during the 1990s was smaller for scheduled castes and particularly scheduled tribes. Among nonscheduled castes, the prevalence of underweight (and severe underweight) was reduced by 14 percent (23 percent) between 1992/93 and 1998/99. Over the same period, the prevalence of underweight (and severe underweight) among scheduled caste groups declined just 7 percent (15 percent); among scheduled tribes, the decline was just 2 percent (9 percent).

Although underweight prevalence is widespread across India, just 10 percent of villages and districts accounted for 27–28 percent of all underweight children in the country. As few as a quarter of districts and villages accounted for more than half of all underweight children (World Bank 2004a) (figure 1.8).

Figure 1.8 In 1998/99, more than half of all underweight children in India lived in just one-quarter of all villages and districts

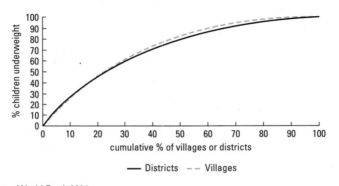

Source: World Bank 2004a.
Note: Villages and districts are ranked by number of underweight children.

The geographic concentration of underweight means that tailoring an appropriate response to malnutrition in a country as large and diverse as India requires a more richly textured picture of malnutrition patterns and trends than the national picture presented above. It also suggests that, where reliable data on malnutrition prevalence are available, actions to combat undernutrition could be targeted to a relatively small number of districts and villages.

The rest of this section examines how the prevalence of and trends in underweight varied across states and across socioeconomic groups within states in 1992/93 and 1998/99. Since data from only two points in time are used, it cannot be assumed that these trends represent longer-term changes in undernutrition.

Interstate and Within-State Variation

Variation by State The prevalence of underweight and the extent to which it fell (or occasionally rose) during the 1990s varied widely across states (table 1.5). Underweight prevalence in Bihar and Madhya Pradesh fell from 60 percent to about 55 percent during the 1990s. As

Table 1.5 Prevalence of underweight, 1992/93 and 1998/99, by state

Item	Below-average prevalence (less than 47 percent)	Above-average prevalence (at least 47 percent)
Increase in malnutrition	Manipur (28; 4)	Orissa (55; 4) Rajasthan (51; 14)
Below-average reduction in malnutrition (0–11.6 percent)	Gujarat (46; –6) Haryana (35; –2) Himachal Pradesh (45; –2) Kerala (27; –0.5) Mizoram (28; –1)	Madhya Pradesh (55; –8) Maharashtra (50; –3) Tripura (50; –6) Uttar Pradesh (52; –10)
Above-average reduction in malnutrition (more than 11.6 percent)	Andhra Pradesh (38; –20) Arunachal Pradesh (25; –35) Assam (37; –27) Delhi (35; –16) Goa (29; –16) Jammu and Kashmir (35; –19) Karnataka (44; –13) Meghalaya (38; –15) Nagaland (24; –14) Punjab (29; –37) Tamil Nadu (37; –22)	Bihar (55; –12) West Bengal (49; –14)

Source: Calculated from NFHS I (1992/93) and NFHS II (1998/99) data.
Note: First figure in parentheses refers to prevalence in 1998/99; second figure refers to the change in prevalence between 1992/93 and 1998/99.

a result, by 1998/99 no state in India had a malnutrition prevalence exceeding 60 percent.

In six states—Bihar, Madhya Pradesh, Maharashtra, Orissa, Rajasthan, and Uttar Pradesh—however, at least half of children were underweight in 1998/99. A combination of large populations and high underweight prevalence means that four of these states—Bihar (11 percent), Madhya Pradesh (11 percent), Rajasthan (10 percent), and Uttar Pradesh (11 percent)—accounted for 43 percent of all under-weight children in India (World Bank 2004a). Most of these high-prevalence states also experienced the smallest reductions in the prevalence of underweight, with Orissa and Rajasthan registering sharp increases in underweight prevalence.

Variation by Location In all states except Tripura, the percentage of underweight children was higher in rural areas than in urban areas (figure 1.9). The magnitude of these differentials varied. The largest percentage differences between rural and urban areas were observed in Jammu and Kashmir (81 percent), Punjab (78 percent), West Bengal (64 percent), and Delhi (61 percent). Although Manipur, Orissa, and Rajasthan were the only states that registered increases in total underweight prevalence between 1992/93 and 1998/99, Delhi registered significant increases in the prevalence of rural malnutrition, and

Figure 1.9 Urban-rural disparities in underweight among children, by state, 1992–9

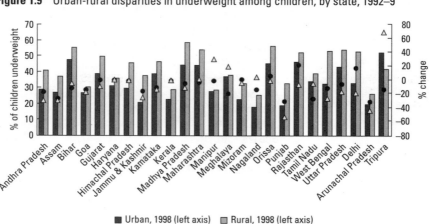

■ Urban, 1998 (left axis)　■ Rural, 1998 (left axis)
▲ Urban, 1992–8 (right axis)　● Rural, 1992–8 (right axis)

Source: Calculated from NFHS I (1992/93) and NFHS II (1998/99) data.

the northeastern states of Manipur, Meghalaya, Nagaland, and Tripura experienced increases in urban malnutrition.[7]

Variation by Gender At the national level, the prevalence of underweight among girls exceeded the prevalence of underweight among boys by more than 3 percentage points, and the rate of decline in the prevalence of underweight among boys was about 2.3 times that of girls (see figure 1.7). This pattern of gender disparities did not characterize every state. Indeed, while the national trend was echoed in Assam, Bihar, Gujarat, Karnataka, Kerala, Madhya Pradesh, Meghalaya, West Bengal, and Uttar Pradesh, in other states, such as Goa, Jammu and Kashmir, Mizoram, Nagaland, and Tripura, the prevalence of underweight fell more among girls than among boys. In the three states in which total underweight prevalence increased (Manipur, Orissa, and Rajasthan), the increase for both girls and boys was equal.

In some states one gender has remained consistently disadvantaged relative to the other; in others gender disparities have worsened over time. In Delhi and Orissa, the percentage of underweight boys has been consistently higher than the percentage of underweight girls, while the reverse has been true of Punjab, Tamil Nadu, and West Bengal (table 1.6). In other states, such as Jammu and Kashmir, girls were in a worse position than boys in 1992/93 but not in 1998/99. In Assam, Bihar, Karnataka, Kerala, Madhya Pradesh, Rajasthan, and Uttar Pradesh, girls fared better than boys in 1992/93, but by 1998/99 they had lower nutritional status.

Table 1. 6 Classification of states by change in gender differentials in prevalence of underweight

Item	States
Percentage of underweight girls exceeds percentage of underweight boys in both 1992/93 and 1998/99.	Andhra Pradesh, Gujarat, Haryana, Manipur, Punjab, Tamil Nadu, West Bengal
Percentage of underweight boys exceeds percentage of underweight girls in both 1992/93 and 1998/99.	Arunachal Pradesh, Goa, Delhi, Orissa, Nagaland, Tripura
Percentage of underweight girls exceeds percentage of underweight boys in 1998/99 but not 1992/93.	Assam, Bihar, Karnataka, Kerala, Madhya Pradesh, Meghalaya, Rajasthan, Uttar Pradesh
Percentage of underweight boys exceeds percentage of underweight girls in 1998/99 but not 1992/93.	Himachal Pradesh, Jammu and Kashmir, Mizoram

Source: Calculated from NFHS I (1992/93) and NFHS II (1998/99) data.

Variation by Caste The national pattern in which the prevalence of underweight is highest among scheduled tribes, followed by scheduled castes and then other castes, obscures variations at the state level. Consistent with the national pattern, underweight prevalence in 1998/99 was higher among scheduled castes in Arunachal Pradesh, Himachal Pradesh, Jammu and Kashmir, Nagaland, and Tripura. But in Assam, Goa, and Manipur, the underweight prevalence was higher among other castes than among scheduled tribe and scheduled caste groups.

Within each state, the trend in underweight prevalence varied dramatically across castes. In Gujarat, Maharashtra, Tripura, and Uttar Pradesh, for example, the underweight prevalence of scheduled tribes increased while the underweight prevalence of other scheduled and nonscheduled castes declined. A similar pattern was observed for scheduled castes relative to other castes in Himachal Pradesh and Kerala.

Variation by Wealth With almost no exceptions, the prevalence of underweight, in both 1992/93 and 1998/99, was much higher among relatively poor households than among relatively well-off ones (figure 1.10).[8] A troubling finding is that the aggregate reduction in the prevalence of underweight between 1992/93 and 1998/99 was smaller for the lowest tertile (poorest third) than for the upper tertile (richest

Figure 1.10 Change in prevalence of underweight, by wealth tertile and state, 1992–8

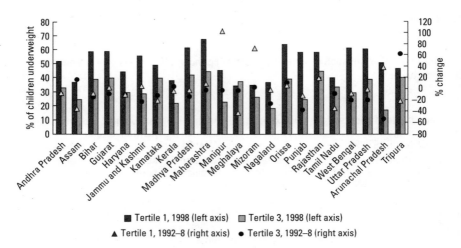

■ Tertile 1, 1998 (left axis)　▨ Tertile 3, 1998 (left axis)
▲ Tertile 1, 1992–8 (right axis)　● Tertile 3, 1992–8 (right axis)

Source: Calculated from NFHS I (1992/93) and NFHS II (1998/99) data.
Note: Manipur data have very few observations in tertile 1 in 1992. Tertile 1 is the poorest, tertile 3 is the richest.

third). This was true not only in aggregate but also in most states in India, indicating growing disparities in the prevalence of underweight among the well off and the not so well off. This trend was not universal: in a few states (such as Assam, Tamil Nadu, and Tripura) the percentage reduction in underweight prevalence among the lower tertile was much greater than among the upper tertile, indicating some narrowing of nutritional inequalities (table 1.7).

Prevalence of Micronutrient Deficiencies

The main micronutrient deficiencies in India are iron deficiency anemia, Vitamin A deficiency, and iodine deficiency disorders.

Iron Deficiency Anemia

Prevalence Although prevalence figures vary from study to study, there is no doubt that iron deficiency anemia is an extremely serious public health problem in India, especially among pregnant women and children. At least half of all ever-married women 15–49 and adolescent girls are believed to have some degree of iron deficiency anemia (IIPS

Table 1.7 Wealth disparities in the change in underweight prevalence, by state, 1992/93 and 1998/99

Item	States
Growing intertertile nutritional inequalities as a result of	
malnutrition declined less in tertile 1 than tertile 3	Andhra Pradesh, Bihar, Madhya Pradesh, Nagaland, Punjab, West Bengal, Uttar Pradesh
malnutrition increased in tertile 1 and declined in tertile 3	Arunachal Pradesh, Gujarat, Jammu and Kashmir, Maharashtra, Manipur
malnutrition increased more in tertile 1 than tertile 3.	Mizoram, Rajasthan
Narrowing intertertile nutritional inequalities as a result of:	
malnutrition declined less in tertile 3 than tertile 1	Karnataka, Meghalaya, Tamil Nadu
malnutrition increased in tertile 3 and declined in tertile 1	Assam, Kerala, Tripura
malnutrition increased more in tertile 3 than in tertile 1.	Orissa

Source: Calculated from NFHS I (1992/93) and NFHS II (1998/99) data.

and Orc Macro 2000; Anand, Kant, and Kapoor 1999; Singh and Toteja 2003). One study shows that the prevalence of iron deficiency anemia among both pregnant and lactating women exceeds 75 percent and that more than half of pregnant women and a third of lactating women are moderately or severely anemic (NNMB 2002). In some states an anemia prevalence as high as 87 percent has been found among pregnant women from disadvantaged groups (IIPS and Orc Macro 2000; Seshadri 2001; Kapil and others 1999). Severe anemia from iron deficiency is believed to claim the lives of 22,000 women during pregnancy and childbirth each year (UNICEF 2003b).

The prevalence of iron deficiency anemia among children is much higher than among adult women and may be partly attributable to the high prevalence of hookworm among children. The overall prevalence of anemia among children 6–35 months is 74 percent, with most suffering from mild (23 percent) or moderate (46 percent) anemia (IIPS and Orc Macro 2000). Prevalence among children 1–5 years is a little lower, but two-thirds of these children can be classified as anemic, with the majority suffering from moderate anemia (NNMB 2002).

Trends Very little progress was made in reducing the prevalence of iron deficiency anemia between 1990 and 2000 (figure 1.11). Moreover, population growth added 34.1 million non-pregnant and 2.3 million pregnant anemic women during this time period (Mason, Musgrove, and Habicht 2003). Although the prevalence of iron deficiency anemia among preschool children fell somewhat, from almost 80 percent in 1990, it remained high, at about 75 percent, in 2000 (UNICEF and MI 2004b). By contrast, the prevalence of iron deficiency anemia in Bangladesh and Pakistan fell to 55 percent within the same period, and in China, the prevalence of iron deficiency anemia fell more than 60 percent (from more than 20 percent to the current level of 8 percent).

Variation by Demographic and Socioeconomic Characteristics The prevalence of moderate iron deficiency anemia among children 6–35 months varies greatly by demographic and socioeconomic characteristics (figure 1.12). It tends to be higher among children from disadvantaged groups—rural children, children living in poor households, and children from scheduled castes and tribes. The prevalence of mild anemia (about 23 percent) and severe anemia (about 5 percent) varies less with demographic and socioeconomic characteristics. There is almost no difference in the prevalence of iron deficiency anemia by gender.

Figure 1.11 Trends in prevalence of iron deficiency in preschool children, by world region, 1990, 1995, and 2000

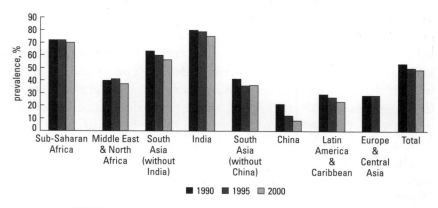

Source: UNICEF and MI 2004b.

The pattern of iron deficiency anemia among ever-married women 15–49 is similar to that among children, but the variation is larger. The total prevalence among women from scheduled tribes and the poorest 20 percent of the population, for example, was at least 10 percentage points higher than the national average of 52 percent. Iron deficiency anemia is a condition that afflicts not only the poor: more than 40 percent of women in the richest two quintiles were also anemic.

Figure 1.12 Prevalence of anemia among children 6–35 months and women of reproductive age, by demographic and socioeconomic characteristics, 1998/99

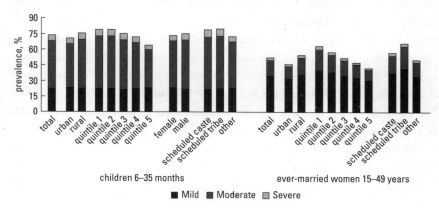

Source: IIPS and Orc Macro 2000.

Interstate Variation The prevalence of iron deficiency anemia varies widely across states, among both children and ever-married women. While fewer than one-half of children in Kerala, Manipur, and Nagaland were anemic in 1998/99, more than 80 percent of children in Bihar, Haryana, Punjab, and Rajasthan were. The prevalence of child anemia was generally higher in states with a high prevalence of underweight, although some states with a relatively low underweight prevalence (such as Punjab and Sikkim, where fewer than one-third of children are underweight) had a surprisingly high prevalence of iron deficiency anemia (80 percent in Punjab and 77 percent in Sikkim).

The variation in iron deficiency anemia prevalence among ever-married women was even greater, ranging from 23 percent in Kerala to 70 percent in Assam. Manipur (29 percent), Goa (36 percent), and Nagaland (38 percent) also had relatively low prevalence. By contrast, in seven states—Arunachal Pradesh, Assam, Bihar, Meghalaya, Orissa, Sikkim, and West Bengal—more than 60 percent of ever-married women were anemic. In some states, such as Arunachal Pradesh and Assam, the prevalence of iron deficiency anemia among women was even higher than that among children under 3. (For figures on the prevalence of iron deficiency anemia among women and children disaggregated by state and severity of iron deficiency anemia, see appendix table A.2.)

Vitamin A Deficiency

Prevalence The prevalence of Vitamin A deficiency in India is one of the highest in the world, especially among preschool children, among whom 31–57 percent suffer from subclinical Vitamin A deficiency and another 1–2 percent suffer from clinical Vitamin A deficiency (UNICEF and MI 2004b; West 2002). India is home to more than one-fourth of the world's preschool children suffering from subclinical Vitamin A deficiency (35.4 million of 127.3 million) and one-third of preschool children with xerophthalmia (1.8 million of 4.4 million) (ACN/SCN 2004). Nationwide, Vitamin A deficiency is estimated to precipitate the deaths of more than 300,000 children a year (UNICEF and MI 2004a).

Vitamin A deficiency is also prevalent among women of reproductive age, among whom clinical symptoms of night blindness are extremely widespread. About 1 in every 20 pregnant women has subclinical Vitamin A deficiency, and almost 12 percent of them suffered from night blindness during their most recent pregnancy (West

2002). An extremely high prevalence of maternal night blindness, coupled with a large number of pregnancies, means that about half of the world's pregnant woman with night blindness live in India (3 million of 6.2 million). As might be expected, the prevalence of night blindness is much higher in rural areas (14 percent) than in urban areas (6 percent) (IIPS and Orc Macro 2000).

Trends Some progress has been made in reducing Vitamin A deficiency in India, but the prevalence of subclinical Vitamin A deficiency remains one of the highest in the world (figure 1.13). Prevalence fell rapidly in the early 1990s, to less than 60 percent among preschool children, but progress slowed in the second half of the 1990s. Recent estimates place the current prevalence at about 57 percent (UNICEF and MI 2004b; Mason and others 2003).

Interstate Variation There is huge variation in the prevalence of Vitamin A deficiency among children across states. The incidence of vision problems can be used as an indicator of Vitamin A deficiency (figure 1.14).[9] The number of children with vision problems is less than 10 per 1,000 children in several states and union territories, such as Gujarat and Punjab, but in many states in the North East, such as Assam, Manipur, Mizoram, Sikkim and Tripura, as well as in Goa, Jammu and Kashmir, and West Bengal, more than 30 per 1,000 children have vision problems (DWCD and UNICEF 2001).

Figure 1.13 Changes in prevalence of subclinical Vitamin A deficiency among children under 6, by world region, 1990, 1995, and 2000

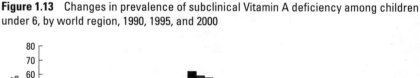
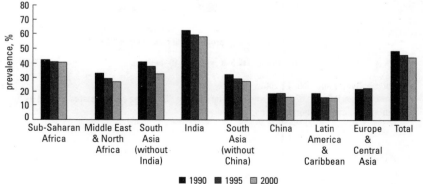

Source: UNICEF and MI 2004b.

Figure 1.14 Proportion of children experiencing daytime and nighttime vision difficulties

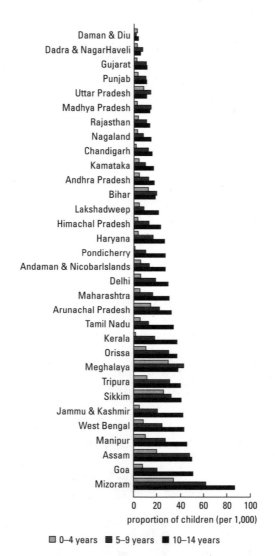

□ 0–4 years ■ 5–9 years ■ 10–14 years

Source: DWCD and UNICEF 2001.
Note: The variation in day-time and night-time vision difficulties across states is used as an indicator of the variation in Vitamin A deficiency.

Iodine Deficiency Disorders

Prevalence Although the prevalence of iodine deficiency disorders in India is lower than in most South Asian countries, the problem is ubiquitous and affects millions of people (figure 1.15). One survey shows that more than 85 percent of districts (241 of 282) are iodine deficiency disorder endemic (Ministry of Industry 2000). This places about 329 million people at risk, equivalent to one-third of India's population or one-sixth of the total global population at risk of iodine deficiency disorder. Among those who suffer from iodine deficiency disorder in India, 51 million are school-age children (6–12 years). One-third of all children in the world that are born with mental damage related to iodine deficiency disorder live in India (Ministry of Industry 2000; ACC/SCN 2004).

Interstate Variation As with other vitamin and mineral deficiencies, the prevalence of iodine deficiency disorder varies widely across and within states. During the 1980s, 17 states and most hilly regions were identified as goiter endemic (Gopalan 1981). More recently, new endemic areas appear to have emerged in the plains (WHO 2000). According to a five-state study conducted in 2001, the prevalence of

Figure 1.15 Prevalence and number of iodine deficiency disorders in the general population, by world region and country

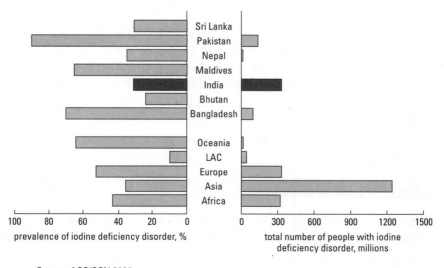

Source: ACC/SCN 2004.
LAC = Latin America and the Caribbean.

iodine deficiency disorder ranged from 15 percent in Tamil Nadu to 46 percent in Karnataka. At the district level, the variation is even greater: for example, the East Godavari and Nellore districts of Andhra Pradesh, and the Kannur district of Kerala are effectively free of iodine deficiencies, while the prevalence is as high as 90 percent in the Shimoga district of Karnataka (WHO 2004a).

Will India Meet the Nutrition MDG?

The MDGs are a set of internationally agreed goals that countries and institutions have committed to reach by 2015. The first MDG is to eradicate extreme poverty and hunger. The second target of this MDG—halving the proportion of the population suffering from hunger between 1990 and 2015—uses two indicators to measure progress: the prevalence of underweight among children under 5 and the proportion of the population below a minimum level of dietary energy consumption.

Several studies, using different assumptions, have considered the likelihood that India will attain the MDG target (see, for example, Wagstaff and Claeson 2004; Chhabra and Rokx 2004; World Bank 2004a).[10] Although their projections differ, all of these studies conclude that it is unlikely that the prevalence of malnutrition in India will fall from its level of 54 percent in 1990 to 27 percent by 2015 (World Bank 2004a).[11] National Family Health Survey (NFHS) data show that in 1998/99, even the wealthiest quintile had a prevalence of malnutrition (33 percent) that far exceeded the MDG target. This report's projections indicate that economic growth alone is unlikely to be sufficient to lower the prevalence of malnutrition. When combined with policy interventions, the projections are rosier, but a rapid scaling-up of health, nutrition, education, and infrastructure interventions is needed if the MDG is to be met (World Bank 2004a).

Effect of Economic Growth Alone

The effect that India's economic growth in the coming decade will have on the prevalence of malnutrition in 2015 can be projected using estimates of the responsiveness (elasticity) of malnutrition to annual economic or income growth. The magnitude of these elasticities should ideally be calculated from household surveys (Haddad and others 2003), provided that they include appropriate income or expenditure data. In the absence of these data, an alternative is to assume a rule-of-thumb elasticity and test its sensitivity.

Two assumptions are made in order to estimate the effect that economic growth will have on the prevalence of underweight. The first is that India's economy will grow at an annual rate of 3 percent, the average rate between 1990 and 2002 (World Bank 2004b). The second is that the income elasticity of underweight is 0.51 (Mkenda 2004). This means that a 1 percent increase in per capita GDP leads to a 0.51 percent reduction in the prevalence of underweight.

Under these assumptions, the prevalence of underweight among children under 3 falls to 39 percent by 2015 (table 1.8 and figure 1.16). Under a more generous average annual per capita growth rate of 5 percent, prevalence falls to 36.3 percent—still short of the MDG target. Even under an unrealistically generous income elasticity assumption of 0.7, prevalence falls only to 35 percent (under the assumption of 3 percent growth) or 30 percent (under the assumption of 5 percent growth). Under the assumption that the prevalence of underweight in 2002 has fallen somewhat since 1999 (for example, by 1 percent a year to 43 percent), the change in the predicted prevalence is greater, but it still remains far in excess of the 27.4 percent mark. Only when an exceptional average annual per capita economic growth rate of 8 percent is assumed does underweight fall low enough to reach the MDG target. This sensitivity analysis shows that the conclusion that economic growth alone will not enable India to meet the MDG target is robust to a wide range of assumptions.

Table 1.8 Under all likely economic growth scenarios, India will not reach the nutrition MDG without direct nutrition interventions

Estimated prevalence of underweight in 2002 (percent)	Income elasticity of malnutrition	Prevalence of underweight among children under 5, given various average annual per capita GDP growth rates (percent)		
		3 percent	5 percent	8 percent
43	0.51	35	31	
47	0.51	39	36	27.3
47	0.3	41	39	
47	0.7	35	30	

Note: See appendix table A.1 for calculations.

Figure 1.16 Predicted prevalence of underweight under different economic growth scenarios, 2002–15

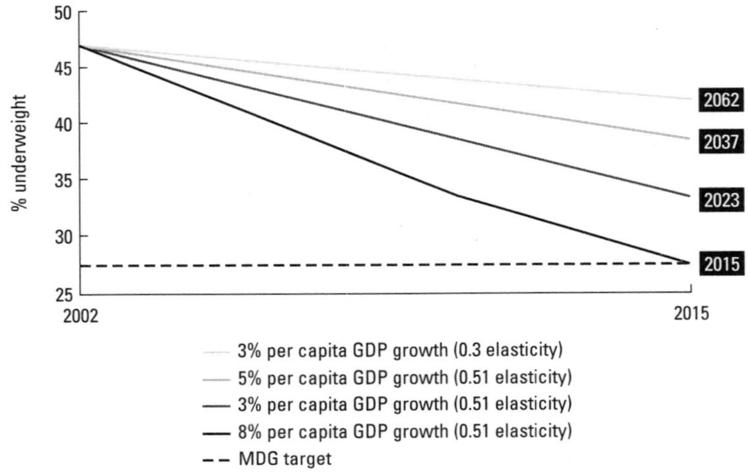

Source: World Bank calculations.
Note: Boxed years at the right of the graph denote the predicted date that the MDG target will be met.

Effect of Economic Growth Plus an Expanded Set of Interventions

Projections from a recent World Bank study (World Bank 2004a) combine economic growth assumptions and policy interventions. They show that even if poor states were brought up to the national average in terms of sanitation, road access, electricity, medical attention at time of delivery, female schooling, household income (consumption), and public spending on nutrition per child, the cumulative reduction in the national prevalence of underweight would be only about 8 percentage points (or 15 percent). If the magnitude of the proposed interventions were scaled up to bring the poor states up to the average level prevailing in the nonpoor states, the cumulative reduction in the prevalence of underweight rate would be 21 percentage points, or 38 percent—still short of the MDG target. Only when seven specific interventions are pursued simultaneously is the prevalence of child underweight in the poor states expected to fall 25 percentage points—enough for them to reach the target figure (figure 1.17).[12]

Figure 1.17 Projected percentage of children under 3 in poor states who are underweight, under different intervention scenarios, 1998–2015

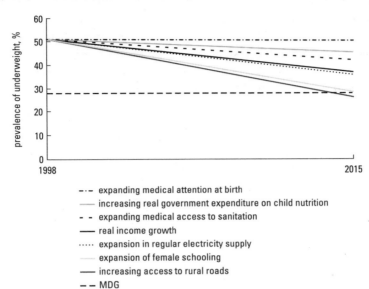

Source: World Bank 2004a.

Conclusions

The problem of undernutrition in India is of alarming magnitude and great complexity. The prevalence of underweight is among the highest in the world—nearly twice that in Sub-Saharan Africa—and the pace of improvement lags behind what might be expected given India's economic growth. Modest progress has been made in reducing undernutrition over the past decade, but most of this progress was driven by improvements among higher socioeconomic groups. Even if India comes close to achieving the nutrition MDG in 2015 (which it most likely will not), it will still have levels of undernutrition equivalent to those that exist in Sub-Saharan Africa today (Shekar and others 2004).

Aggregate levels of undernutrition are extremely high, and significant inequalities across states and socioeconomic groups appear to be growing. Girls, children in rural areas, children from the poorest households, and children from scheduled tribes and castes are the worst affected. In

Bihar, Madhya Pradesh, Maharashtra, Orissa, Rajasthan, and Uttar Pradesh, more than half of all children are underweight. Thus, while undernutrition is a national problem, the problem is more acute among certain groups. Immediate action needs to be taken to address malnutrition, using strategies that take into account local variations in nutritional status and the fact that certain demographic and socioeconomic groups are more vulnerable to malnutrition than others.

CHAPTER 2

The Integrated Child Development Services Program

Are Results Meeting Expectations?

India's primary policy response to child malnutrition, the Integrated Child Development Services (ICDS) program, is well conceived and well placed to address the major causes of child undernutrition in India. Some important mismatches between its policy intentions and actual implementation are preventing it from reaching its full potential, however. More attention has been given to increasing coverage than to improving the quality of service delivery; too few children under 3, for whom malnutrition prevention is most critical, are being reached; and too much emphasis is being placed on distributing food rather than changing family-based feeding and care behavior. The program also faces substantial operational challenges.

The ICDS has expanded tremendously over its 30 years of operation to cover almost all development blocks in India. It offers a wide range of health, nutrition, and education services to children, women, and adolescent girls. The program was intended to target the poorest, the most undernourished, and the age groups that represent a significant "window of opportunity" for nutrition investments (that is, children under 3 and pregnant and lactating women). There is a mismatch, however, between the program's intentions and its actual implementation:

- The central focus on food supplementation drains financial and human resources from other tasks envisaged in the program that are crucial for improving child nutritional outcomes. For example, not enough attention is given to improving childcare behaviors or educating parents about how to improve nutrition.

- Older children (3–6 years) participate much more than younger children, and many children from poorer households do not yet participate. The program fails to preferentially target girls, children from lower castes, or children from the poorest villages, all of whom are at higher risk of undernutrition.

- Although program growth was greater in underserved than well-served areas during the 1990s, the poorest states and those with the highest levels of undernutrition still have the lowest levels of program funding and coverage by ICDS activities.

In addition to these mismatches, the program faces substantial operational challenges. Inadequate worker skills, shortages of equipment, poor supervision, and weak monitoring and evaluation reduce the program's potential impact. Community workers are overburdened because they are expected to provide preschool education to 4- to 6-year-olds as well as nutrition services to all children under 6. As a result, most children under 3—the group that is most vulnerable to malnutrition—do not receive micronutrient supplements, and most of their parents are not reached with counseling on better feeding and childcare practices.

Successful interventions have taken place in many districts, and innovations and variations in the ICDS have occurred in several states. These successes, described in the last section of this chapter, suggest that the potential for better implementation and greater impact exists.

How ICDS Aims to Address the Causes of Persistent Undernutrition

With strong government commitment and political will, the ICDS program has emerged from a small pilot in 1975 to become India's flagship nutrition program. Many of the ICDS program components are well designed to address the immediate causes of child undernutrition in India, although significant shifts in focus and improvements in implementation will be necessary if the program is to realize that potential.

A Conceptual Framework of the Causes of Undernutrition

Child undernutrition is a consequence of complex interactions among multiple determinants. These interactions can be conceptualized using a framework that traces the causal pathways of undernutrition through different levels: the most immediate, the underlying, and the basic causes (figure 2.1).

Immediate Causes of Undernutrition The most immediate causes of malnutrition are inadequate dietary intake and infections, which create a vicious cycle that is responsible for much of the high morbidity and mortality among children in developing countries. When children do not consume enough, their immune response is lowered, rendering them more susceptible to infectious diseases. Ill children deplete their nutritional stores and are in poor health because of reduced intake,

Figure 2.1 Causes of child malnutrition

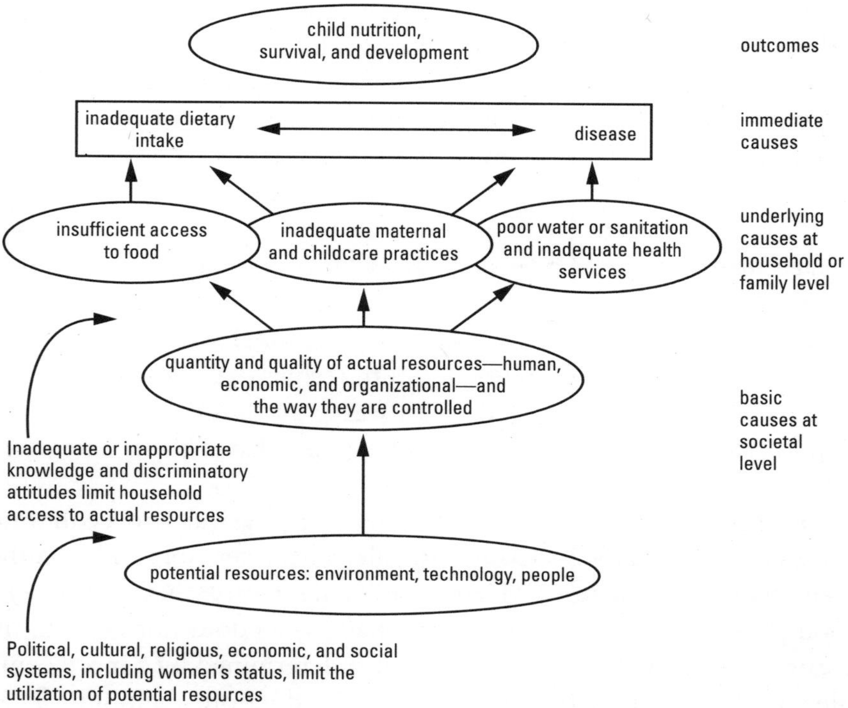

Source: UNICEF 1998.

poor absorption of nutrients, and the increased demands of combating disease (Esrey and others 1990; Scrimshaw and SanGiovanni 1997; Allen and Gillespie 2001).

Over the past decade, a large body of work has documented the interaction between nutrition and infection. Evidence of the malnutrition-infection syndrome was first reported in studies conducted in Guatemala and India. These studies found that children developed diarrheal infections around the time of weaning from breastmilk and that they were subsequently more prone to infections and growth faltering (Gordon and others 1964; Scrimshaw and others 1968). While the weight loss associated with a single episode of infection can be made up if the diet is adequate, recurrent episodes of infection without sufficient food or inadequate recovery time are primary causes of poor growth among children in developing countries (Schürch and Scrimshaw 1989). Following infection, a number of weeks pass before the child's weight returns to the pre-onset level, retarding the child's growth. In the case of diarrhea, the degree of growth deficit has been shown to be proportional to the number of days ill (Martorell and others 1975). If infections are frequent, high rates of underweight prevail even when food intake is adequate. The converse is also true: if infections are less common or less severe, lower rates of child undernutrition prevail even if average food intake is low. Thus, sufficient food intake is only one determinant of nutritional status.

Underlying Causes of Undernutrition The two immediate causes of malnutrition, poor dietary intake and infection, are closely linked to the three underlying determinants of nutritional status: household-level access to food, availability of health resources (such as preventive and curative health care and clean water and sanitation), and the appropriateness of the childcare and feeding behaviors that caregivers adopt.[1]

Household-level food security refers to physical and economic access to foods that are socially and culturally acceptable and of sufficient quality and quantity. Macro-level food security (that is, sufficient food production at national or regional levels) does not necessarily ensure household-level security, which is determined by a more complex array of factors than agricultural production, including local prices (of food and other goods), income, and an effective trade and transport infrastructure (Bouis and Hunt 1999). Moreover, household food security is not in itself sufficient to ensure that the nutritional needs of every child, and adult, living in a particular household will be met. Within each household, decisions are made as to the quantity and quality of food that is allocated to each household member. This decision is affected by a complex range of factors, including the relative bargaining power of household members (which in turn may be related to their income, autonomy, gender, and education), as well as other characteristics, such as the health status of individual members. Consequently, the diets of individual children (or others) within the household may be deficient even though per capita caloric intake is high and the household is food secure.

Overcrowding, congestion, a shortage of clean water, and inadequate facilities for the disposal of human excreta, wastewater, and solid waste contribute to the development of gastrointestinal infections such as diarrhea, and facilitate the spread of infectious disease. This explains why mortality rates in urban areas exceeded those of rural areas before the sanitation revolution but were lower than rural rates after it (Collins and Thomasson 2002).

Crowding has been shown to be associated with an increased risk of infectious intestinal disease (due to rotavirus group A) in children (Sethi and others 2001) and tuberculosis infection (MacIntyre and others 1997). Poor water quality, a limited quantity of water, poor excreta disposal practices, and poor food hygiene are all associated with an increased prevalence of diarrhea in infants (Esrey and others 1990; Moe and others 1991). Clean water, good sanitation, and hygienic conditions at the community level generate important externalities for individual households in the community: clean water and good sanitation at the neighborhood level have been shown to have a positive effect on the height of children in a household, whether or not the household itself has a healthy environment (Alderman and others 2003).[2]

The presence of infection, particularly communicable disease, is a direct cause of malnutrition. Consequently, efforts to prevent exposure to infection and cure disease should be central to any strategy aimed at combating malnutrition. These efforts include regular deworming, the use of bed nets in malaria areas, oral rehydration therapy, and access to regular and affordable health check-ups.

Providing appropriate care can mitigate the impact of the malnutrition-infection cycle for vulnerable groups, such as children and pregnant and lactating women. Such care requires adoption of childcare and feeding behaviors that direct available resources toward promoting child nutritional well-being. Adequate care during pregnancy and delivery can reduce the incidence of maternal death, miscarriage, stillbirth, and low birth weight among infants. Adequate feeding of young children (initiation of breastfeeding within an hour of birth, exclusive breastfeeding for the first six months of life, and adequate and timely complementary feeding starting at six months while continuing to breastfeed) is critical for child growth. Caregivers' time, their knowledge and educational status, autonomy, control over monetary and other resources, and capacity to make appropriate decisions are often the key factors that determine whether these behaviors are adopted.

Basic Causes of Undernutrition The framework shown in figure 2.1 links these underlying determinants to a set of basic determinants, including the availability of human, economic, and organizational resources with which to improve nutrition. Use of these resources is shaped by how society is organized in terms of economic structure; political and ideological expectations; and the institutions through which activities and resources within society are regulated, social values are met, and potential resources are converted into actual resources.

The Design of the ICDS Program and the Underlying Causes of Child Undernutrition

The ICDS program is potentially well poised to address some of the underlying causes of persistent undernutrition. The program adopts a multisectoral approach to child well-being, incorporating health, education, and nutrition interventions (table 2.1), and is implemented through a network of *anganwadi* centers at the community level. These centers range from open-air spaces to *anganwadi* workers' homes to one- or two-room stand-alone buildings. The Department of Women and Child Development's emphasis on a life-cycle approach means that malnutrition is fought through interventions targeted at unmarried adolescent girls, pregnant women, mothers, and children from birth to 6 years. Services provided include health

Table 2.1 Range of services that the ICDS seeks to provide to children and women

	Children under 6	Pregnant women	Lactating women
Health check-ups, and treatment	Health check-ups by AWW, ANM, LHW Treatment of diarrhea Deworming Basic treatment of minor ailments Referral for more severe illnesses	Antenatal check-ups	Postnatal check-ups
Growth monitoring	Monthly weighing of under-threes Quarterly weighing of 3- to 6-year-olds Weight recorded on growth cards		
Immunization	Immunization against poliomyelitis, diphtheria, pertussis, tetanus, tuberculosis, and measles	Tetanus toxoid immunization	
Micronutrient supplementation	IFA and Vitamin A supplementation for malnourished children	IFA supplementation	
Health and nutrition education		Advice includes infant feeding practices, child care and development, utilization of health services, family planning, and sanitation	Advice includes infant feeding practices, child care and development, utilization of health services, family planning, and sanitation
Supplementary nutrition	Hot meal or ready-to-eat snack providing 300 calories and 8g–10g protein Double rations for malnourished children	Hot meal or ready-to-eat snack providing 500 calories and 20g–25g protein	Hot meal or ready-to-eat snack providing 500 calories and 20g–25g protein
Preschool education	Early Childhood Care and Preschool Education consisting of "early stimulation" of under-threes and education "through the medium of play" for children aged 3–6 years		

Source: DWCD 2004a.

check-ups, treatment and referral for infants and children, growth monitoring, immunization, micronutrient supplementation, supplementary feeding, preschool education for children 3–6, and health and nutrition education for adult women. As the program has developed, it has expanded its range of interventions to include components focused on adolescent girls' nutrition, health awareness, and skills development, as well as income-generating schemes for women.

ICDS and the World Bank

Total government expenditure on ICDS has grown significantly since the program's inception. Following expenditure of about 1,190 Indian rupees (Rs1,190) *crores* (1 *crore* equals 10 million) during its first 17 years (1975–92), the government increased spending from Rs2,271 *crores* under the Eighth Five-Year Plan (1992–7) to Rs4,557 *crores* under the Ninth Five-Year Plan (1997–2002) (DWCD 2005). The Tenth Five-Year Plan (2002–7) allocates Rs10,391 *crores* to the program. In addition, the program has been supported by several donors, including UNICEF, the Swedish International Development Cooperation Agency, the World Food Programme, Care, and the Norwegian Agency for Development Cooperation.

The World Bank has supported efforts to improve nutrition in India since 1980 through six projects. With an investment of $712.3 million in the sector, India accounts for the largest share of Bank Group lending devoted specifically to nutrition programs. Support to ICDS has been provided in three overlapping phases:

- In Phase I the Bank supported the Tamil Nadu Integrated Nutrition Project (TINP) as an alternative to the standard ICDS program in the state of Tamil Nadu (TINP I, 1980–9; TINP II, 1990–7).

- In Phase II support was extended to the standard government ICDS programs, as well as to some additional activities (ICDS I in Orissa and Andhra Pradesh, 1991–7; ICDS II in Bihar and Madhya Pradesh, 1993–2000).

- In Phase III the primary emphasis moved from expanding coverage to improving the quality of services (through an ICDS component in the Andhra Pradesh Economic Restructuring Program, 1999–2004, and the Woman and Child Development Project, 1999–2004).[3]

Empirical Findings on the Impact of ICDS

The ICDS program has been the subject of a large volume of research. Most evaluations have focused on the quality of infrastructure and inputs and the execution of activities. Few rigorous studies have evaluated the program's impact on nutritional status or health behaviors, partly because few data sources permit outcomes among program participants and non-participants to be compared. Consequently, most researchers have been unable to use the statistically rigorous methodologies that would enable them to draw reliable conclusions about the impact of ICDS. Some studies have found that the program is associated with improvements in nutritional status, while others have failed to find a positive effect. It is not clear to what extent the failure to reach consensus is the result of inadequate survey design and poor data quality. In the future, to be sure of measuring the impact accurately, it will be necessary to collect data on treatment and control populations, preferably over at least two time periods.

The major national-level study of program impact (NIPCCD 1992) found that the prevalence of underweight was lower among children in areas in which the ICDS program was in place, for both children under 3 and children 3–6.[4] Because of the small sample sizes of the control and treatment groups, however, both these differences are statistically insignificant (Lokshin and others 2005).

Three recent studies have estimated the association between having an *anganwadi* center in a village and the likelihood that a child is underweight. All three find little or no association between the presence of a center and child nutritional status. Using multivariate analysis of the 1992/93 National Family Health Survey (NFHS) data, the World Bank (2004a) estimates that, for boys, having an *anganwadi* center is associated with a 5 percent reduction in the likelihood of being underweight but that there is no significant association for girls. Using both the 1992/93 and the 1998/99 NFHS data, Lokshin and others (2005) initially find that ICDS appears to have a significant and positive effect on nutritional outcomes, but on more rigorous exploration, using propensity score matching techniques, they find little significant effect when children in ICDS villages are compared with children with similar demographic, household, and village characteristics in non-ICDS villages. In a multivariate model of cross-sectional data collected in Kerala, Rajasthan, and Uttar Pradesh between 2000 and 2002, Bredenkamp and Akin (2004) find that children in villages with *anganwadi* centers are not significantly less likely to be underweight or ill than other children. Using data from Chhattisgarh, Kerala, Madhya Pradesh, Maharashta, Rajasthan, and Uttar Pradesh, they find that only in Kerala is actual attendance at an *anganwadi* center significantly associated with better nutritional status.

There is little evidence that ICDS has been successful in attaining its goal of improving the coverage of specific child health interventions, such as deworming and Vitamin A supplementation, or encouraging mothers to adopt appropriate childcare and feeding behaviors (including practices related to breastfeeding, weaning, and diet) that have the potential to improve child growth and health outcomes. Data from Kerala, Rajasthan, and Uttar Pradesh show no clear evidence that these behaviors were more common in ICDS areas; only in Maharashtra was an association found (Bredenkamp and Akin 2004) (table 2.2). Although communication for behavior change through the *anganwadi* worker is a crucial weapon in the fight against poor health and malnutrition, it appears that the information the *anganwadi* worker is conveying to mothers is not being communicated effectively enough to positively affect mothers' behavior.

Targeting of ICDS Program and Beneficiaries

Geographical Targeting: Placement of Programs across States and Villages

The percentage of administrative blocks covered by ICDS has reached almost 90 percent (see appendix table A.3). The percentage of children who actually take up the services provided by the program is lower, however, and varies significantly across states (figure 2.2). By December 2002, only one-quarter of all Indian children between the ages of 6 months and 6 years were benefiting from the supplementary nutrition component of ICDS, with the figure ranging from little more than 10 percent in some states to more than 90 percent in others.[5] Coverage is particularly high in the northeastern states.

ICDS policy stipulates that one *anganwadi* center should be in place per 1,000 population, with more intensive placement of 1 per 700

Table 2.2 Comparison of intermediate health outcomes and behaviors across children living in villages with and without an *anganwadi* center

	In villages	Kerala	Maharashtra	Rajasthan	Uttar Pradesh
Percentage over 6 months receiving Vitamin A supplementation	No AWCs	81.2	80.5	29.8	18.0
	with AWCs	78.3***	**88.5***	22.5***	**21.0***
Percentage older than 12 months ever dewormed	No AWCs	61.1	34.3	3.7	17.7
	with AWCs	**66.3***	**59.7***	4.1	13.3***
Percentage over 6 months consuming Vitamin A–rich food within previous 3 days	No AWCs	78.1	78.1	27.6	36.0
	with AWCs	72.0***	**90.5***	26.9	32.5***
Percentage breastfed within 1 hour of delivery	No AWCs	85.6	54.4	9.4	6.1
	with AWCs	80.0***	41.2***	10.3	6.7
Percentage consuming colostrum	No AWCs	98	8.9	74.1	53.4
	with AWCs	96.9***	**28.7***	**80.4***	37.3***
Percentage under 6 months who are exclusively breastfed	No AWCs	67.1	21.5	38.4	99.7
	with AWCs	58.2***	11.3***	**43.3***	84.6***
Percentage aged 6–9 months consuming complementary food	No AWCs	84.1	67.3	93.8	0.3
	with AWCs	87.7	**73.6**	93.7	**19.1***
Mean duration of breastfeeding, among children who have been weaned (in months)	No AWCs	13.4	16.3	8	23.7
	with AWCs	12.5***	17.4***	7.1***	22.8***

Source: Calculated from ICDS III baseline/ICDS II endline survey 2000–2.
Notes: * statistically significant at the 10% level; ** 5% level; *** 1% level; AWC = *anganwadi* center.
For clarity, **boldface** indicates where outcomes are significantly better in villages with AWCs.

population in tribal areas, where poverty tends to be more prevalent. In practice, ICDS centers are much more numerous in wealthier states (figure 2.3). States with lower per capita net state domestic product have a smaller percentage of villages covered by the ICDS program than those with higher per capita net state domestic product. The growth of program coverage from 1992 to 1998 was more rapid in the poorest villages, however (Lokshin and others 2005).

Regardless of the indicator of ICDS coverage used (percentage of villages with a center, number of ICDS beneficiaries, public expenditure on ICDS), access to the program appears to be worst in the poorest states and in the states with the worst nutrition indicators (figure 2.4). The five states with the highest underweight prevalence (Rajasthan, Uttar Pradesh, Bihar, Orissa, and Madhya Pradesh) rank in the bottom 10 in terms of ICDS coverage.

Figure 2.2 The percentage of children 6 months to 6 years enrolled in the supplementary nutrition program, 2002, varies widely across states

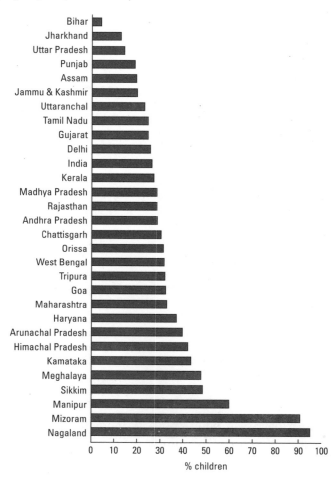

Source: Department of Women and Child Development enrollment data (updated 2004); Census of India (2001).

Note: Figures are calculated from Department of Women and Child Development data on the number of children between the ages of 6 months and 6 years who were beneficiaries of the Supplemental Nutrition Program in December 2002 and from population data for children under 6 in 2001. The use of different age categories may result in a slight underestimation of the percentage of beneficiaries, while the use of population data from 2001 may result in a slight overestimation of the percentage of beneficiaries. The magnitude and direction of the bias are hard to predict.

Figure 2.3 ICDS coverage is higher in states with higher per capita net domestic product

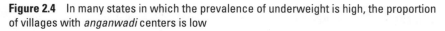

Source: Coverage calculated from NFHS II (1998/99) data; net state domestic product data are from Indiastat.com.
Note: Data are in current prices for 1998/99.

Village-level data reveal that ICDS placement is less regressive within than across states. In 1998, for example, while ICDS was in place in only half of the villages in the lowest two deciles of the all-India wealth distribution, the program covered about 80 percent of the richest villages in India. The difference in program coverage between the poorest and the wealthiest villages within each state was much smaller: about 60 percent of the poorest villages in every state

Figure 2.4 In many states in which the prevalence of underweight is high, the proportion of villages with *anganwadi* centers is low

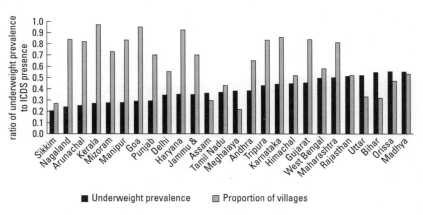

■ Underweight prevalence   ▨ Proportion of villages

Source: Underweight prevalence calculated from NFHS II (1998–9); appendix table A.3.

were covered by the ICDS program, compared with 70 percent of the wealthiest villages (Lokshin and others 2005).

The percentage of children enrolled in the ICDS program tends to be smaller in states with a higher percentage of underweight children (figure 2.5). Enrollment is lowest in Bihar (1.5 percent), where the underweight prevalence is 55 percent. At the other end of the spectrum, Manipur, Mizoram, Nagaland, and Sikkim exhibit an underweight prevalence that is among the lowest in India (20–30 percent) but are among the five states with the highest percentage of ICDS beneficiaries. The clear exception to this pattern is Orissa, which has a very high underweight prevalence (47 percent) but has enrolled at least 95 percent of children in the program.

The states in which the prevalence of malnutrition is highest are also the states that receive the least funding from the central government and the smallest financial allocations from the state governments for ICDS. Government per child expenditure in support of states' ICDS programs appears to be strongly and inversely proportional to the states' underweight prevalence.

In addition, the (per child) amount allocated by state governments to ICDS—most of which is spent on the supplementary feeding component—is lowest in the states with the highest underweight prevalence and highest in the states with the lowest underweight prevalence. Total public expenditure figures show that four of the

Figure 2.5 Fewer children are enrolled in ICDS in states in which the prevalence of underweight is high

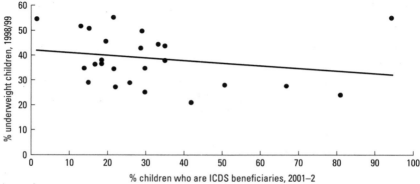

Source: Calculated from NFHS II (1998/99), DWCD (2003), and 2001 Census of India data.

states that rank in the top five for underweight prevalence (Bihar, Uttar Pradesh, Rajasthan, and Madhya Pradesh) are also the four states that receive the least funding for ICDS, on a per child basis.[6] This regressive relationship holds true at the other end of the spectrum, too, where the five largest per child allocations are made to and by the five states that have the lowest underweight prevalence (figure 2.6). Since poorer states find it difficult to mobilize resources for ICDS, the government of India has recently proposed providing additional central financing to all states to cover half of the cost of the supplementary nutrition component.

Individual Targeting: Characteristics of Beneficiaries

Effective targeting restricts nutrition interventions to those individuals or groups that are most vulnerable to malnutrition. In so doing, it maximizes the social returns and minimizes costs. However, the high generalized malnutrition prevalence in India and the administrative costs associated with excluding those who are relatively well-off means that rigorous targeting of ICDS benefits to particular socioeconomic groups is unlikely to prove feasible. Instead, ICDS policy

Figure 2.6 Public expenditure by state and national governments is very low in states in which the prevalence of underweight is very high

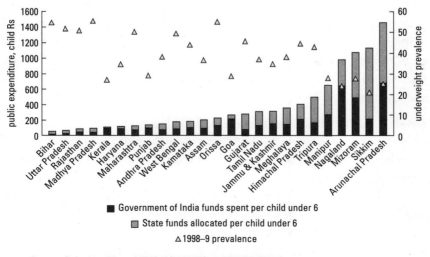

■ Government of India funds spent per child under 6
▨ State funds allocated per child under 6
△ 1998–9 prevalence

Source: Calculated from NFHS II (1998/99) and DWCD (2003).

Figure 2.7 Older children are more likely than younger children to attend an *anganwadi* center

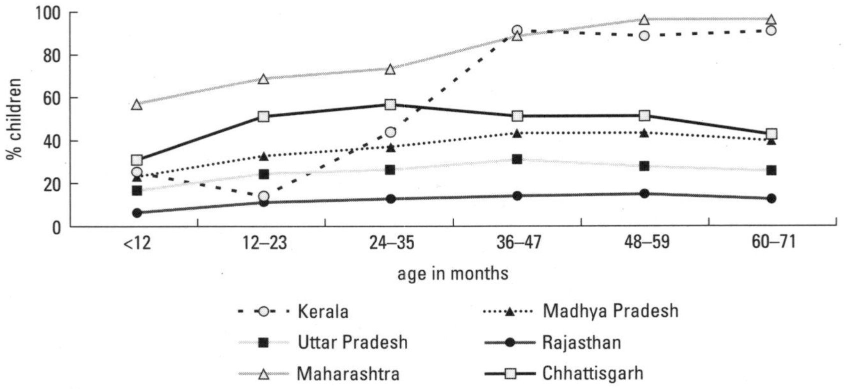

Source: ICDS III baseline/ICDS II endline survey 2000–2.
Note: Data show percentage of children in villages with *anganwadi* centers who attend a center at least once a month.

follows the general guideline that a "special effort" should be made to reach children from lower-income families or scheduled tribes and castes. There is also some explicit targeting of severely malnourished children, who are supposed to receive double food rations.

This section examines whether children who are most in need of the ICDS program have access to its services and use them on a regular basis. It presents the findings of a survey on children's attendance at *anganwadi* centers in Chhattisgarh, Kerala, Madhya Pradesh, Maharashtra, Rajasthan, and Uttar Pradesh during 2000–2 (henceforth referred to as the ICDS III baseline/ICDS II endline survey).[7] The data are disaggregated by age, gender, caste, household wealth, and location.

Targeting by Age Early childhood is a crucial developmental period, during which there is considerable scope to influence the growth of malnourished children. However, it is precisely this group of children—infants and children under 3—that is least likely to attend the *anganwadi* center. Attendance is lowest among the youngest children, increasing steadily—sometimes dramatically—until the age of 3, after which it remains more or less constant (figure 2.7). In Kerala and Maharashtra, almost every child 4–6 in the sample attended the center at least once a month. Attendance rates were less than half of that in the other four

Figure 2.8 The caste and tribe composition of children attending *anganwadi* centers varies somewhat across states

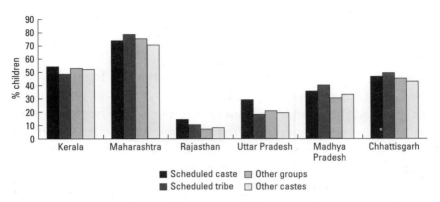

Source: ICDS III baseline/ICDS II endline survey 2000–2.
Note: Data show percentage of children in villages with *anganwadi* centers who attend a center at least once a month.

states. When daily, rather than monthly, attendance figures are examined, the gap between the attendance rates of children under 3 and children 4–6 is much larger (see appendix figure A.2).

Targeting by Gender Neither daily nor monthly attendance figures reveal a statistically significant difference in the participation rates of boys and girls. There appears to be no gender discrimination in the reach of ICDS services.

Targeting by Caste The ICDS scheme places special emphasis on the participation of children of lower castes. Some *anganwadi* centers have been constructed in close proximity to scheduled caste and scheduled tribe colonies, and *anganwadi* workers are expected to take steps to encourage the recruitment of these children into the program.

In all states, attendance rates of children from scheduled castes and tribes are in line with or slightly higher than those of children from other castes (figure 2.8). In Chhattisgarh, Madhya Pradesh, and Maharashtra, the percentage of children from scheduled tribes attending a center is higher than any other caste, while in Kerala, Rajasthan, and Uttar Pradesh, the percentage of children from scheduled castes is higher than that of children from other castes. These data are supported by qualitative evidence of high take-up among scheduled tribes relative to forward castes, perhaps partly because of the social stigma associated with the receipt of benefits among the upper castes (Educational Resource Unit 2004). Caste composition differs from center to center, with attendance by children of a particular caste apparently influenced by the caste of the *anganwadi* worker and the caste that is most dominant in the local community.

Targeting by Household Wealth Among children living in villages with *anganwadi* centers, remarkably little variation is found in participation rates across wealth quintiles: within each state, there is not much more than a 10 percentage point difference across wealth quintiles (figure 2.9). This implies that a poor economic background does not present too formidable an obstacle to ICDS attendance. But since poorer children are more likely to be malnourished, it is desirable that ICDS attracts a larger share of lower quintile than upper quintile children. Maharashtra is the only state in which attendance declines steadily as wealth increases. In Chhattisgarh and Uttar Pradesh, attendance is slightly lower in the top quintile; in Kerala and Madhya Pradesh, attendance is more regressive, with higher attendance rates in the upper quintiles. A similar picture is obtained when one examines daily attendance figures: with the exception of Maharashtra, the percentage of upper quintile children attending centers is either as high as or higher

Figure 2.9 The percentage of children who attend *anganwadi* centers varies only slightly across wealth quintiles

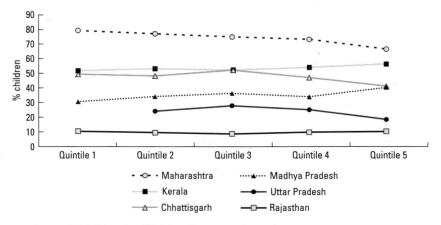

Source: ICDS III baseline/ICDS II endline survey 2000–2.
Note: Data show percentage of children in villages with *anganwadi* centers who attend a center at least once a month. Quintile 1 is the poorest quintile, quintile 5 is the richest.

than the percentage of lower quintile children (see appendix table A.4 for figures).

These state-level enrollment figures may obscure low enrollment among economically disadvantaged children in specific villages. Field visits to Uttar Pradesh, for example, found that the poorest of the poor were frequently excluded from ICDS interventions and under-represented at *anganwadi* centers (Educational Resource Unit 2004).

Targeting by Urban-Rural Location There is much heterogeneity across states in attendance rates of children living in urban, rural, and tribal areas (figure 2.10). In Chhattisgarh and Madhya Pradesh, for example, attendance rates are highest in urban areas, followed by tribal areas, while in Kerala and Uttar Pradesh attendance rates are highest in rural areas.

Summary Although large proportions of vulnerable groups are indeed taking up the ICDS benefits for which they are eligible, there is substantial program capture by the less needy—possibly at the expense of more vulnerable children. Attendance by lower castes is relatively high, but there is still scope to attract a greater percentage of this group. Additional effort needs to be made to reach younger children and children from poor households, who are not only underrepresented at *anganwadi* centers but also at greatest risk for malnutrition.[8]

Figure 2.10 Attendance at *anganwadi* centers varies widely both across and within states

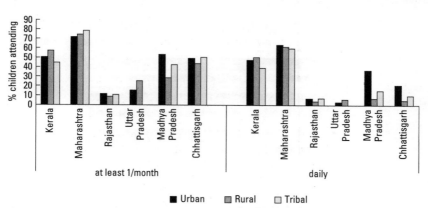

Source: ICDS III baseline/ICDS II endline survey 2000–2.

Characteristics and Quality of ICDS Service Delivery

Promoting growth and providing supplementary food are central to the ICDS objective of reducing the prevalence of malnutrition. This section examines the delivery of these services, especially with respect to the availability of equipment and supplies and the frequency with which these services are delivered. It also looks at the quality of *anganwadi* center infrastructure, the training and competencies of *anganwadi* workers, and the coordination between the ICDS and the Reproductive and Child Health Program.

Promoting Growth

Growth-monitoring activities are hampered by poor access to appropriate equipment, such as scales, growth cards, and wall or book charts. Equipment is often nominally present but not of sufficient quantity or quality. *Anganwadi* centers in Kerala and Madhya Pradesh are generally better equipped than those in Chhattisgarh, Maharashtra, and Uttar Pradesh, although they, too, suffer equipment shortages (figure 2.11). Even in centers with working scales, many workers report that they do not weigh children under 3 every month. In all states, growth-monitoring performance appears to be superior in tribal areas, where children are weighed with greater frequency.

Figure 2.11 Percentage of *anganwadi* centers with growth-monitoring equipment in place

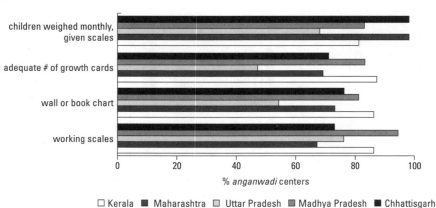

% *anganwadi* centers

□ Kerala ■ Maharashtra □ Uttar Pradesh ▨ Madhya Pradesh ■ Chhattisgarh

Source: ICDS III baseline/ICDS II endline survey (2000–2).

Anganwadi centers in urban and tribal areas are better equipped with weighing equipment than rural centers.

Even with regular weighing, growth monitoring is effective only if accompanied by communication for behavior change that results in improved growth of the malnourished child. Previous studies of ICDS have noted that this does not often occur, perhaps because many *anganwadi* workers are not fully competent in interpreting growth cards and curves (Gopalan 1992) or because *anganwadi* workers fail to effectively communicate the meaning of children's growth patterns to mothers (Vasundhara and Harish 1993). Indeed, the ICDS III baseline/ICDS II endline survey reveals a very large discrepancy between the child's measured weight and the mother's subjective assessment of her child's growth status. In Kerala, all mothers think their children are experiencing normal growth; in Uttar Pradesh, where underweight prevalence in the ICDS III baseline/ICDS II endline sample is 46 percent, 94 percent of women describe their children's nutritional status as normal.

Providing Supplementary Nutrition

The Supplementary Nutrition Program is one of the best-known ICDS interventions. Food is financed and procured by the states and provided to children at the center, either in the form of a ready-to-eat snack or a meal cooked by the *anganwadi* worker. Many children receive food at the center, with state averages ranging from about 20–80 children per center, depending on the center's location. In addition, in most states there is a take-home food component, from which about 20–25 children per center benefit.

Despite the resources and energy devoted to it, the supplementary nutrition program appears to perform poorly, especially in terms of providing a regular supplementary source of nutrition to the needy while simultaneously excluding the non-needy. Irregularities in the food supply and leakage to non-targeted individuals are major problems (table 2.3).

The most commonly reported reasons why children do not receive supplementary food from the *anganwadi* center relate to inadequacies on the supply side. In decreasing order of importance, these include lack of availability of food for distribution, lack of awareness of the food program among mothers or a failure to realize that their children

Table 2.3 Regularity of food supply to AWCs and the availability of the take-home food program

	Kerala	Maharashtra	Uttar Pradesh	Madhya Pradesh	Chhattisgarh
Percentage of AWCs with no recent irregularities in food supply	60	41	68	27	17
Percentage of AWCs with a take-home food program	15	28	42	95	75

Source: ICDS III baseline/ICDS II endline survey 2000–2.

are eligible for the program, failure of the *anganwadi* worker to contact mothers or children when food is available, and the distance of the *anganwadi* center from children in need.[9]

These findings strongly suggest that ICDS needs to improve the regularity of the food supply. Indeed, in three of the five states surveyed in 2000–2, the majority of *anganwadi* centers reported irregularities in their food supply during the preceding three months. Another evaluation reported that 27 percent of *anganwadi* centers experienced disruptions in food distribution for periods of more than 90 days (NIPCCD 1992).

There is also some evidence that household attitudes and behaviors are important determinants of children's access to ICDS food. Some mothers think that their children do not need the food (even though the same children have been assessed by researchers as malnourished). Other mothers fail to collect the food from the *anganwadi* center, sometimes because their families prohibit them from doing so. Large-scale household surveys reveal negligible complaints about food quality or quantity (Bredenkamp and Akin 2004), but field visits have shown that food is sometimes badly cooked, dry, and salty (Educational Resource Unit 2004) and should be supplemented by sugar, rice, or vegetables, perhaps procured locally, to be more palatable to children.

Leakage of supplementary food to nontargeted beneficiaries appears to be widespread. In many states, attendance rates among children from relatively wealthy households are higher than those among children from relatively poor households. In practice, there appears to be little targeting of children from disadvantaged groups for supplementary feeding or of malnourished children for double rations of supplementary food. Food is often distributed to all those who come to the center (Educational Resource Unit 2004). Where the center is located on school premises, food is distributed to grade 1 children as well as preschool children, so that the number of beneficiaries often exceeds the number of children actually enrolled at the center. As a result, children often receive less than the recommended 300 kilocalories of food. In some instances, food is also distributed to indigent adults, and it is common for *anganwadi* helpers, and occasionally *anganwadi* workers, to take cooked food home (Educational Resource Unit 2004).

There is substantial leakage in the take-home food component of ICDS, since many children share the food with siblings or elders. In Madhya Pradesh, for example, only about a third of children consume all take-home food themselves. One-third of children consume less than a quarter of the food, and 6 percent consume none of the food taken home from the center (Bredenkamp and Akin 2004). Most *anganwadi* workers surveyed describe the take-home food component as "not useful."

The supplementary nutrition program is effective as an incentive to attract children to the centers, where they can then receive other health- and nutrition-related services; without the program, attendance at the centers might be much lower. Community-based monitoring mechanisms have recently been introduced in some areas in an attempt to improve the delivery of supplementary nutrition.

Providing a Safe and Hygienic Environment for ICDS Service Delivery

Growth promotion, the provision of supplementary food, and the delivery of other ICDS services are sometimes performed in unsafe or unhygienic environments. Most centers in urban areas (but not those in rural areas) are located in rented buildings (table 2.4), especially community buildings, such as primary schools, religious centers, and *panchayat* buildings. While potentially improving community scrutiny of ICDS, use of these buildings may render the regular functioning of the center vulnerable to the competing purposes for which these buildings are used. Moreover, because the budgetary allocation to rent is low, *anganwadi* centers may be found in small or unclean locations. Some ICDS centers are run out of the homes of ICDS functionaries.

About one-third of *anganwadi* centers in India have *pucca* (brick and mortar–type construction buildings), another third have semi-*pucca*

Table 2.4 *Anganwadi* center (AWC) infrastructure, by location

	Kerala			Maharashtra			Uttar Pradesh		Madhya Pradesh			Chhattisgarh		
	Urban	Rural	Tribal	Urban	Rural	Tribal	Urban	Rural	Urban	Rural	Tribal	Urban	Rural	Tribal
Percentage of AWCs with drinking water that is														
piped or pumped	69	44	50	21	44	41	54	70	100	58	83	73	83	72
open well	27	41	17	0	20	34	0	8	0	0	0	0	4	0
other	4	15	33	79	36	25	46	22	0	42	17	27	13	28
Percentage of AWCs with toilets that are														
flush	27	15	0	0	2	0	8	7	50	19	14	36	13	16
pit-latrine	20	26	0	0	13	10	29	10	8	15	7	9	9	4
none	53	59	100	100	85	90	63	84	42	65	79	55	78	80
Percentage of AWCs with rented building	64	41	50	96	19	41	92	15	92	46	21	82	17	44
Number of AWCs in sample	45	27	6	24	54	29	24	61	12	15	29	11	23	25

Source: ICDS III baseline/ICDS II endline survey 2000-2.

construction, fewer than one-third are in *kutcha* buildings (buildings constructed with low-quality materials, such as unburned brick, bamboo, thatch, or mud roofing); a handful of centers function in open spaces, such as under trees (NCAER 2001). Cooking space is typically inadequate, as reported by 55 percent of *anganwadi* workers across the country (NCAER 2001). Most *anganwadi* centers have no toilet facilities, especially in rural and tribal areas.[10] Among centers with toilets, flush toilets are more common in urban areas and pit-latrines are more common in rural and tribal areas. The majority of *anganwadi* centers obtain their drinking water from a tap or hand pump, but the water source varies substantially across state and rural-urban-tribal location.

Worker Training, Workload, and Status

The skills of the *anganwadi* worker and her capacity to mobilize the community to support ICDS and recruit participants, especially the most vulnerable, are central to good-quality service delivery and effectiveness. Too often performance is constrained by poor training and the pressure of a large and diverse workload.

Skills Training Anganwadi workers tend to be well educated, but they are often poorly trained for ICDS tasks. Survey data show that almost all have at least matriculated high school, and half of those in urban areas have received some college education. Pre-service training is rare, however, with most women undergoing only short-term in-service training (Bredenkamp and Akin 2004). Recently, more resources have been directed toward strengthening capacity at the central, state, and block levels to provide high-quality support and training to functionaries of ICDS programs.

In 2002, a new training program, *Udisha* ("first rays of the new dawn"), was initiated, with funding from the World Bank. This program has attempted to shift the focus of training away from the mere transfer of knowledge toward the strengthening of worker competencies.

Workload, Status, and Remuneration Anganwadi workers can spend up to 40 percent of their time on supplementary nutrition–related activities and another 39 percent on preschool education (NCAER 2001). This leaves little time for other important ICDS activities, such as growth promotion, health and nutrition education, home visits, referral services, and meeting with the community. In addition, *anganwadi* workers must maintain at least 10 different types of records.[11] *Anganwadi* workers are also often given other responsibilities outside of ICDS. When *anganwadi* centers are located on school premises, for example, some workers have the additional responsibility of teaching class (grade) 1 (Educational Resource Unit 2004). In some communities, *anganwadi* workers are required to meet family planning and sterilization targets. *Anganwadi* workers are also called on to assist in other government programs for women and children, such as the Pulse Polio campaign. Home visits—to advise on antenatal care and promote breastfeeding, timely immunization, and regular weighing—appear to be one of the more neglected of ICDS tasks, with only 78 percent of *anganwadi* workers in Maharashtra, 68 percent in Chhattisgarh, 43 percent in Madhya Pradesh, 38 percent in Uttar Pradesh, and 35 percent in Kerala undertaking the equivalent of at least one home visit a day (Bredenkamp and Akin 2004).

Despite the importance of their work, *anganwadi* workers are often held in low regard by the community (Educational Resource Unit 2004), viewed as "mere" providers of child care rather than valuable healthcare workers. There are also frequent lags in payment of honoraria. According to ICDS III baseline/ICDS II endline survey 2000–2, as many as two-thirds of urban *anganwadi* workers in Uttar Pradesh report that they do not receive their honoraria regularly. The low status the community attaches to the position of *anganwadi* worker, and the irregularity with which workers are paid reduces workers' motivation.

Collaboration between ICDS and the Reproductive and Child Health Program

The objectives of the Reproductive and Child Health Program and ICDS are intertwined; the promotion of linkages between the activities of the two programs would therefore be mutually beneficial. Already some of these linkages are recognized in the job descriptions of *anganwadi* workers and auxiliary nurse-midwives. *Anganwadi* workers are supposed to promote awareness of national immunization days and maintain immunization records, refer sick children to healthcare facilities, and encourage mothers to seek antenatal care. Auxiliary nurse-midwifes, employed by the Department of Health, are supposed to conduct general health check-ups of ICDS beneficiaries, give immunizations, dispense medicines and contraceptives, and provide assistance and guidance to *anganwadi* workers in the discharge of their health-related duties.

In practice, cooperation between the ICDS and the Reproductive and Child Health Program appears to be limited, partly because of the absence of a designated person or body to oversee the promotion of this collaboration. Site visits reveal that *anganwadi* workers take little interest in finding out whether mothers are registered with the auxiliary nurse-midwife and receiving antenatal care, and the ICDS III baseline/ICDS II endline survey (2000–2) shows that visits to *anganwadi* centers by auxiliary nurse-midwifes are not very regular. In Kerala, for example, only 50 percent of urban centers and no rural centers had received a visit from an auxiliary nurse-midwife the previous month (Bredenkamp and Akin 2004).[12] As a result, it is perhaps not surprising that some *anganwadi* workers, and as many as one-third of those surveyed in rural Uttar Pradesh, are inclined to believe that the auxiliary nurse-midwife does not perform significant services during her visits. The fact that the provision of health services is not consistently better in villages with *anganwadi* centers than in villages without them seems to suggest that there is little coordination or convergence between the two. Deworming is more frequent in villages with *anganwadi* centers in Kerala and Maharashtra but not in Rajasthan and Uttar Pradesh. More children receive Vitamin A supplementation in villages with *anganwadi* centers than without *anganwadi* centers in Maharashtra and Uttar Pradesh but not in Kerala or Rajasthan. Although the immunization function is being performed with some regularity (at least 80 percent of *anganwadi* centers in Chhattisgarh, Kerala, Madhya Pradesh, and Maharashtra have immunization registers that have been regularly used), previous studies suggest that ICDS has had little to do with any improvements in immunization coverage (see for example, Kulkarni and Pattabhi 1988).

Although many centers face problems, some are overcoming them to provide very valuable services to their communities. One example is the center in the Bellary district of Karnataka (box 2.1).

Monitoring and Evaluation

A strong monitoring and evaluation system helps program managers track whether project implementation is proceeding as desired and

Box 2.1   Getting things right in the Bellary District of Karnataka: A report from the field

Venkatamma, an *anganwadi* worker, is quick to list the characteristics of a good center.* "It should be a spacious place with clean surroundings, the building should have good ventilation, enough play materials and teaching aids, a mirror for the children to come and have a look, a small garden in front of the center, and they should be received with love," she says. She pauses and then continues with a grin, "Of course, most of these things are not there in my center, but children attend regularly in good numbers." According to Venkatamma, it is the relationship with the children, a good preschool component, and food that attract children to the center.

Venkatamma and her helper, Rankamma, belong to scheduled castes and live close to the center. The center has its own building, with a 12' × 20' classroom, a storeroom, and a kitchen. There are enough vessels for cooking and serving; the water tank is very close to the center, although supply is erratic and water sometimes has to be fetched from a bore-well nearby. A toilet has recently been built, although no one has yet used it.

By and large, Venkatamma's pride in her center was validated by a site visit to the facility. Forty-seven children were present when the Bank team visited, unannounced. By about 10:30 in the morning, the children trooped in, some marching in confidently, others brought in crying by grandmothers or older siblings. The center's staff weigh the children regularly, mark their weight in registers, explain to mothers how the children's growth is progressing, and make suggestions on how to increase their growth. Sometimes, two adolescent girls from the village help run the center.

Venkatamma and Rankamma work well together, and the entire community appreciates and respects them. Women often visit the center to informally interact with them. Mothers were able to describe pregnancy risks and how children should be breastfed. It seems as if the center has acquired a status on a par with the school, where parents send their children regularly.

The center follows a program determined for the week by the state-level authorities. All children are made to wash their hands before they eat; in other *anganwadi* centers in the same village, they even use soap to do so. The children are constantly reminded not to touch the floor or dirty their hands before eating. Venkatamma reported that in her 14 years of service she had never experienced any major gaps in the supply of food, that there was always something for the children to eat. If the supply of rice were delayed, there would be sprouted green-gram or energy food ready for the children. This was confirmed by mothers.

Venkatamma and the health unit coordinate well with each other. She refers problem health cases to the health center, and many mothers now voluntarily bring their children there. Mothers take their children to the *anganwadi* center on immunization days, with the result that immunization coverage is good.

*Names have been changed.

Source: Educational Resource Unit 2004.

make informed decisions to correct any problems. Periodically, it allows an assessment to be made of the extent to which the program is having the desired impact. In so doing, monitoring and evaluation promotes the most effective and efficient use of resources.

Some notable accomplishments have occurred in monitoring and evaluation in recent years. The current system nevertheless faces many challenges. Given the size of the ICDS program, monitoring and evaluating is a daunting task.

A standardized data collection procedure is employed in all states, but it is complex and for the most part relies on manual entries and compilations. Each *anganwadi* worker maintains as many as 10–25 different registers into which information is entered, some of it on a daily basis.[13] Once a month, the *anganwadi* worker compiles this information into a standardized monthly progress report that contains a number of input, process, and impact indicators. These monthly progress reports are then sent to supervisors (each of whom supervises about 20 centers), who consolidate the reports and forward them to the child development project officers, who assemble reports by project-block and remit them to the state headquarters and central ICDS monitoring cell. At the central level, some of the key indicators are analyzed, and quarterly progress reports are prepared for the World Bank–funded states.[14] These reports are used by the Department of Women and Child Development, the Planning Commission, the Health and Family Welfare department, and other departments. States are ranked with respect to progress made, and detailed feedback is sent to state headquarters. However, no feedback is conveyed from the state headquarters to lower levels of program implementation, so that local action is seldom taken in response, thus rendering the feedback system rather ineffective.

In light of the important role that an effective monitoring and evaluation system can play in improving child health, strengthening the monitoring and evaluation system is essential. There have been some significant improvements in some states, in part due to the commitment and effort of the government of India and in part due to the presence of bilateral and international agencies, such as Care, the World Food Programme, and the World Bank.[15] The major impediments that remain must be addressed.

Low Prioritization of Activities

Too little emphasis is placed on monitoring and evaluation, in part due to a poor understanding of what it entails and its potential contribution to program effectiveness. The primary focus of program management (at both the central and state level) seems to be on the timely release of allocations to implementing agencies and the recording of expenditures; very little emphasis is placed on assessing the quality of service delivery and the impact of the program. At the local level, few *anganwadi* workers are aware of the purpose and utility of data collection; they view their data collection tasks as routine, boring, and burdensome. The result is that although the ICDS program is being monitored—in the sense that information on inputs and outputs is regularly collected—the system is not oriented toward using that information to inform action, that is, it is not used to enhance service delivery, improve beneficiary recruitment, or, eventually, modify program design. Consequently, there have been delays and bottlenecks in the replenishment of supplies, the neediest beneficiaries are often not reached, and it is difficult to know which elements of the program are most effective.

Lack of Adequate Personnel

The number of qualified people assigned to monitoring and evaluating ICDS is relatively small at almost all levels of program implementation, and those involved usually handle other tasks as well. Overall responsibility for monitoring ICDS rests with the highest positions in the government (at the director or secretary level), but these officials oversee many other programs as well and face severe time constraints. Vacancies in monitoring and evaluation positions are also a problem, with many positions remaining unfilled for extended periods and frequent personnel turnover at senior levels—a phenomenon that is common throughout the Indian bureaucratic system.

At the field level, positions are more stable, but vacancies and irregular supervision are pervasive. In the sample of blocks included in the ICDS III baseline/ICDS II endline survey (2000–2), supervisors had been appointed to all urban *anganwadi* centers in the sample and were fairly active in ICDS activities (with at least 96 percent of the *anganwadi* centers in five of the six states reporting that they had been visited by supervisors the preceding month).[16] However, 10 percent of all rural *anganwadi* workers were not linked to a supervisor.[17] Moreover, many supervisors did not visit regularly: at least 30 percent of the rural *anganwadi* centers that had supervisors in Chhattisgarh and Uttar Pradesh had not been visited by them during the previous month (Bredenkamp and Akin 2004). A monitoring and evaluation curriculum is included in the training syllabuses for field-level ICDS functionaries, but the value of monitoring and evaluation and the importance of collecting data on key project indicators are typically not adequately communicated.

Inadequate Use of Information Systems and Qualitative Data

The information system, which is central to keeping track and making sense of the huge quantity of data collected, is held back by insufficient use of computer networks. Almost all information collected by *anganwadi* workers, supervisors, and child development project officers and forwarded to the state level is transmitted by hand, with very limited use of computers. Software programs are seldom used to analyze the data collected at the state and central level, except in some of the states covered under World Bank ICDS projects. Lack of computer hardware remains a problem up to the district-block levels, partly due to inadequate financial allocations to monitoring and evaluation.

There is also an inherent quantitative bias in the monitoring system, which comes at the expense of the collection of some qualitative information that could assist in the construction of the causal narratives that explain patterns in the quantitative data. Continuous social assessments, which collect qualitative information through community meetings, focus groups, and open-ended questionnaires, are currently being implemented in the states supported by the World Bank, but they are not used in other states.

If ICDS is to substantially reduce child malnutrition, program managers need a reliable, broad-based, and efficient monitoring and evaluation system that enables them to adjust elements of program implementation and design in order to maximize the returns to nutrition investments. Chapter 3 examines some ways in which the current system could be improved.

Lessons from Successful Innovations

There is encouraging evidence that, with relatively small changes in project priorities and design, the impact of the ICDS program on child nutritional status could be substantially enhanced. This can be seen in studies of the successful implementation and performance of regular ICDS projects as well as in studies of projects that have experimented with modifications to the ICDS program (see, for example, SIDA 2000 and Johri 2004). Adapting the lessons learned from these projects and applying them to other ICDS projects can help ensure that the ICDS has the maximum impact.

Achieving Synergy with the Reproductive and Child Health Program and Using Community Members as Agents of Change: Lessons from INHP II

Care India's Integrated Nutrition and Health Project II (INHP II), now active in nine states, reveals the benefits of targeting behavior change interventions at children under 2 and pregnant women, that is, concentrating energies on those critical periods in the life cycle when the greatest impact on health status can be made (Care India 2004).[18] The program promotes closer convergence between the ICDS program of the Department of Women and Child Development and the Reproductive and Child Health Program of the Department of Health and Family Welfare, and encourages mothers to use reproductive and child health services.[19] The underlying premise of convergence is that by working together these programs are more likely to achieve their shared objectives of reducing infant mortality, combating child malnutrition, and improving the health status of women. An example of this is the facilitation of well-publicized nutrition and health days, during which the *anganwadi* worker (from ICDS) and auxiliary nurse-midwife (from the Reproductive and Child Health Program) provide immunizations to children under 2 and antenatal care (including check-ups, iron and folic acid supplementation, and tetanus toxoid immunization) to pregnant women at the *anganwadi* center. Health talks are another important element of these days; take-home rations of supplementary food (sufficient for a few weeks) are provided as an incentive for attendance. The process of setting up the nutrition and health days is facilitated by the community, by engaging mothers groups, self-help groups, and *panchayati raj* institutions.

Another key INHP activity is the appointment and training of "change agents" within the community. Volunteers assigned to families provide health and nutrition information, promote positive health behaviors, and encourage ICDS participation. Volunteers can be women, men, adolescent girls or boys, or traditional birth attendants, each serving 10–15 families. These agents begin their activities at the birth of the child, if not before, when they advise on appropriate newborn care. They follow up with regular home visits until the child is 2. Many of these visits are timed to coincide with critical periods in the life cycle (for example, weaning). They serve as cues to action at times when mothers should initiate new health behaviors in order to protect their children against undernutrition and disease.

The INHP approach appears to be having a significant effect. Fifty-three percent of pregnant women in the intervention areas received three or more antenatal checkups, compared with 38 percent in the nonintervention areas. Other aspects of antenatal care, such as consumption of iron and folic acid tablets and receipt of tetanus toxoid doses, were also better in the intervention areas (see appendix table A.5). Childcare practices improved substantially, with 65 percent of women in the intervention areas initiating breastfeeding within one hour of delivery, compared with 38 percent in the non-intervention areas. Higher proportions of children in the intervention areas received Vitamin A supplementation and were breastfed exclusively for six months, were introduced to complementary feeding appropriately, given more nutritious complementary foods, and vaccinated against measles by the age of 12 months (see appendix table A.6). There appears to be no difference in behavior by children's gender. Some of the greatest differences between intervention and nonintervention areas are found among people of low socioeconomic status, indicating that this intervention is progressive in its reach.

Using Community-Based Interventions: Lessons from the Dular Program

The Dular program, undertaken by state governments in Bihar and Jharkhand, with the assistance of the United Nations Children's Fund (UNICEF), has developed several innovative approaches to improving early childhood nutrition, care, and development.[20] Active in 8 of 60 districts, it focuses on intensive upgrading of ICDS operations, including the collection of birth weight data and the monitoring of care practices. The program has creatively addressed many of the past failings of the ICDS program in Bihar.

As part of the strategy, the *anganwadi* worker in every targeted village teams up with a small group of local resource people, who are given basic training in nutrition, child care, and hygiene. Once trained, the team visits pregnant women and mothers of newborns in their homes to educate them about safe delivery, breastfeeding, immunization, and other essential care practices during pregnancy and early childhood. Since the team is made up of local people from the community, parents respond positively.

Though still young, Dular appears to be having an impact. An evaluation of 450 households indicates that after one year of intervention there was an 8 percent decline in the prevalence of underweight among children under 3, a 20 percent increase in the use of colostrum feeding within one hour of birth, a 20 percent decline in episodes of diarrhea in children under 3 during the three months before the interview, and a 30 percent increase in the consumption of adequately iodized salt by participating families (Saiyed and Srivastava 2005).

Setting Up Mothers Committees: Lessons from Andhra Pradesh

In 1998 the state of Andhra Pradesh began establishing mothers committees in ICDS villages as a means of integrating ICDS into the community and stimulating demand for improved service quality. Mothers committees are informal committees of eight village members, established in line with the guidelines of the general ICDS program, which requires the formation of a *mahila mandal* (women's group). The groups are registered as committees in order to allow formal participation in ICDS and to enhance their legitimacy and accountability. Members serve three-year terms.

Currently, more than 50,000 committees have been established in 351 development blocks in Andhra Pradesh.[21] Committee members are given three rounds of week-long capacity-building training courses that focus on nutrition, health, education, group formation, and economic empowerment, as well as relevant and state-specific social and legal issues. In collaboration with the state AIDS control society, 20,000 mothers committee members and 10,000 adolescent girls have been trained to serve as "change agents" in promoting HIV awareness and healthy sexual attitudes and behaviors.

The roles and responsibilities of these committees with respect to the ICDS program have evolved considerably over time. Originally, they were involved in the civil works components of the World Bank–assisted ICDS I project (selecting construction sites for *anganwadi* centers, monitoring construction, and releasing funds to cover construction costs). More than 15,000 *anganwadi* buildings were completed under the supervision of mothers committees. Today the range of responsibilities includes recruiting *anganwadi* workers and helpers, paying honoraria, monitoring community-based performance indicators for anganwadi centers, establishing local food units to prepare and distribute supplementary food to the *anganwadi* centers, and ensuring that potential beneficiaries receive services. Mothers committee members may also play an active role in motivating adolescent girls to join bridging courses and skills development programs; encouraging school enrollment, especially among girls who have dropped out; and motivating parents to send children to *anganwadi* preschool.

Evaluation of the mothers committees indicates that the program has potential but needs reinforcing. Only 40 percent of committees are formally involved in the ICDS program, and only 31 percent of all mothers report having heard of the committees. Awareness of the committees is higher in tribal areas (49 percent of women and 34 percent of adolescent girls) than in rural areas (25 percent of women and 15 percent of girls) and urban areas (20 percent of girls). A survey of *anganwadi* workers reveals that the mothers committees are very much appreciated, with three-quarters of respondents describing the functioning of the committees as "good" and another 11 percent as "satisfactory" (World Bank 2003).

To increase the impact of the committees on maternal and child health and nutrition, it has been proposed that their role as change agents be strengthened through further training. Such training would help them promote appropriate infant feeding practices and attendance at *anganwadi* centers.

Another way of increasing the role of the mothers committees as change agents would be to empower the committees to manage aspects of the ICDS system rather than simply helping program staff promote healthy behaviors. Subject to the external monitoring of the outcomes they achieve, such responsibilities could include organizing food distribution, appointing *anganwadi* workers, and improving *anganwadi* center infrastructure.

This effort has sought a much more ambitious role for community participation than the INHP II and Dular programs. Those efforts hinged on involving community members as behavioral change agents. The Andhra Pradesh program tried to involve mothers committees in the actual management of ICDS resources—overseeing civil works and releasing funds for construction costs, managing food preparation and distribution, and recruiting and monitoring *anganwadi* workers. To carry out these tasks effectively, community members need leadership training, support, and supervision, as well as clear designation of power. These requirements need to be explicitly built into the program design.

To perform their tasks effectively, program staff need to know exactly what is expected of them, and they need to be supported in the execution of their tasks by supervisors to whom they can turn for advice and who monitor their activities. In addition, it is important that the tasks that participants are expected to perform not change erratically over time. Shifting expectations, combined with lack of authority and project support, can make it difficult for community members to play an active role in program implementation.

Targeting High-Risk Groups: Lessons from TINP

This variation of the regular ICDS program limited itself to a relatively small number of interventions targeting high-risk groups (Heaver 2002; World Bank 1998). Project activities included regular growth monitoring, nutrition education, and health check-ups for all children. Therapeutic supplementary feeding was provided to moderately and severely malnourished children, children whose growth was faltering (especially children under 3), and high-risk pregnant and lactating women.

The TINP also placed more emphasis than the regular ICDS on training workers, building supervision and managerial capacity, and creating an efficient management and information system. Information was analyzed and fed back into project implementation. For example, after it was discovered that families were not changing the way they fed children under 2, the project targeted more of its information and education to parents of young children. These efforts were successful, as mothers who took part in the project knew much more about good nutrition and health practices than other mothers, they breastfed longer, and fewer of their children needed supplementary feeding.

Community participation was also substantially enhanced. Staff were encouraged to develop active and close collaboration with local women's and girls' groups from the community to effect behavior change in the community. Community members were taught to promote birth weight recording, regular monthly weighing, and spot feeding. They were also encouraged to participate in community assessment, analysis, and problem solving.

The TINP halved the prevalence of severe malnutrition in the villages in which it was implemented (Heaver 2002). It showed that universal feeding was not necessary to achieve substantial nutritional and health gains. The program did not, however, fully meet its objective of reducing moderate malnutrition. The project evaluation concluded that to reduce moderate malnutrition, TINP interventions must focus more on home-based actions and proactive integration of nutrition activities with the health system.

CHAPTER 3

Enhancing the Impact of ICDS

Urgent changes are needed to bridge the gap between the policy intentions of ICDS and its actual implementation. In particular, the three main mismatches need to be resolved, so that the program addresses the most important determinants of malnutrition, effectively encourages the participation of younger children and the most vulnerable segments of the population, and reaches areas in which the prevalence of undernutrition is highest.

ICDS was designed to address the multidimensional causes of undernutrition. As the program expands to reach more and more villages, it has tremendous potential to improve the nutritional and health status of millions of women and children.

The key constraint on the program's effectiveness is the fact that implementation has not followed the original design. Increasing emphasis has been placed on providing supplementary feeding and preschool education to children 4–6, at the expense of other components that are crucial for combating persistent undernutrition. Because of this, most children under 3—the group that suffers most from malnutrition—are not being reached, and most of their parents are not receiving counseling on better feeding and childcare practices.

Realizing the potential of ICDS will require realigning its implementation with its original objectives and design. Several steps are needed:

• Ambiguity over the priority of different program objectives and interventions needs to be clarified immediately.

- Activities need to be refocused on the most important determinants of malnutrition. This means emphasizing disease control and prevention activities, education to improve domestic childcare and feeding practices, and micronutrient supplementation. Greater convergence with the health sector, in particular the Reproductive and Child Health program, would help tremendously in this regard.

- Activities need to be better targeted toward the most vulnerable age groups (children under 3 and pregnant women), and funds and new projects need to be directed to the states and districts with the highest prevalence of malnutrition.

- Supplementary feeding activities need to better target those who need them most, and growth-monitoring needs to be performed with greater regularity, with an emphasis on using it to help parents understand how to improve their children's health and nutrition.

- Communities need to be involved in implementing and monitoring ICDS, in order to bring additional resources into the *anganwadi* centers, improve the quality of service delivery, and increase accountability in the system.

- Monitoring and evaluation activities need strengthening through the collection of timely, relevant, accessible, high-quality information—and this information needs to be used to improve program functioning by shifting the focus from inputs to results, informing decisions, and creating accountability for performance.

Mismatches between Program Design and Implementation

Studies of the ICDS program, including this one, have repeatedly raised concerns about its design and implementation. Three major mismatches in implementation undermine the potential of ICDS to address child undernutrition effectively, efficiently, and equitably.

Mismatch I: Although the design of ICDS recognizes the multidimensional determinants of undernutrition, too much emphasis is currently given to providing food security through the supplementary nutrition program. Not enough attention is given to the most effective interventions for child nutritional outcomes, such as improving childcare behaviors and educating parents on how to improve nutrition using the family food budget.

Mismatch II: Service delivery is not focused enough on the youngest children (under 3), who can potentially benefit most from ICDS interventions. In addition, children from wealthier households participate much more than children from poorer ones, and ICDS is only partially succeeding in preferentially targeting girls and lower castes.

Mismatch III: Although the increase in program coverage was greater in underserved than well-served areas during the 1990s, the poorest states and those with the highest levels of undernutrition still have much lower levels of program funding and coverage than other states.

How Can ICDS Reach Its Full Potential?

In this section a menu of options is proposed to increase the impact of ICDS on the nutritional status of priority groups (table 3.1). It draws on the findings of *Millions Saved: Proven Successes in Global Health* (Levine and the What Works Working Group 2004), which documents 17 cases in which large-scale national, regional, and global efforts have improved health status in developing countries. In order to be labeled successful, these cases had to meet a set of rigorous selection criteria. They had to be of large scale, last at least five years, employ a cost-effective intervention, and have an impact on an important health problem. Although no single recipe emerges from the review of the successful programs, a consistent set of ingredients is found to contribute to success: predictable, adequate funding from both international and local sources; political leadership and champions; technological innovation within an effective delivery system, at a sustainable price; technical consensus about the appropriate biomedical approach; good management on the ground; and effective use of information. In most cases, community participation was also a contributing factor.

ICDS is assessed with respect to these elements of success. It present options that the Department of Women and Child Development could consider for realigning the design and implementation of ICDS in order to improve the program's impact.[34] Particular attention is given to what can be done to fix the three mismatches.

Table 3.1 Menu of options for improving ICDS

Positive feature	Area needing improvement	How to do it
Overall program		
Designed to address the multiple determinants of undernutrition (food security, health services, caring and feeding behaviors).	Mismatch I: Wide gap between original intention and design and actual implementation: food supplementation dominates, at the expense of linkages with health sector and counseling of parents.	Rationalize design and improve implementation: • Define priority objectives. • Identify cost-effective interventions to achieve those objectives. • Implement activities to deliver interventions. • Monitor execution and evaluate impact.
Designed to address intergenerational cycle of undernutrition (that is, pregnant women and young children). Although initial design focus was on children 3–6, over the past decade, design focus shifted toward children 0–3.	Mismatch II: Service delivery remains focused on older children (3–6).	Improve targeting of children under 3 and pregnant women: • Strengthen nutrition and health education activities. • Increase home visits. • Improve targeting of poorest and most vulnerable households. • Introduce mini-*anganwadi* centers (*poriawadis*). • Increase outreach activities.
Designed to target poor states and poor and vulnerable people within these states.	Mismatch III: Per child spending is higher in richer states and in states with lower prevalence of malnutrition. Some of the poorest and most vulnerable groups are not reached.	• Address regressive distribution of financing across states by targeting future expansion to districts and blocks with highest prevalence of malnutrition.

Table 3.1 (*continued*) Menu of options for improving ICDS

Positive feature	Area needing improvement	How to do it
Overall program		
Wide coverage. Strong grassroots presence.	Quality of services is poor.	Develop capacity to deliver all nutrition interventions:
		• Increase external participation in service delivery (for example, mothers groups).
		• Increase synergy with other programs (such as reproductive and child health and primary education).
		• Add a second *anganwadi* worker.
		• Contract private sector for specific activities.
		Optimize use of available resources:
		• Improve skills of *anganwadi* workers and helpers.
		• Introduce supportive supervision.
		• Improve supply of inputs.
		Strengthen focus on results and accountability:
		• Decentralize responsibility and management of program to state governments and *panchayat raj* institutions through performance-based financing.
		• Reform the management information system.
		• Reward performance at all levels of the administration.
		• Strengthen community ownership and enhance accountability to local communities.
		• Involve *panchayat raj* institutions in monitoring service delivery.
	Design is standardized and does not reflect local needs.	Introduce flexibility through bottom-up planning.

(continued on next page)

Table 3.1 (*continued*) Menu of options for improving ICDS

Positive feature	Area needing improvement	How to do it
Food security		
Designed to fill the "food gap" in the intake of young, undernourished children.	Food supplementation is universal and absorbs much of the financial and time resources in the *anganwadi* center.	• Ensure that malnourished children are reached by supplementary nutrition program. • Improve efficiency of procurement and distribution of supplementary nutrition program so that resources can be freed up to strengthen other nutrition interventions.
	Food availability is irregular and quality often poor.	• Improve procurement and distribution of food (by decentralizing procurement of food to community level or contracting with the private sector for food distribution, for example).
	Leakage to non-priority groups	• Strengthen management information systems. • Encourage community ownership and monitoring.
Health		
Designed to link with health services for immunization, Vitamin A supplementation, and referral of high-risk children and pregnant women.	Articulation with health system is weak.	• Strengthen convergence with the Reproductive and Child Health Program. • Introduce joint bottom-up planning process with the Reproductive and Child Health Program. • Provide better training of auxiliary nurse-midwifes in nutrition issues and best practices.
	Emphasis on counseling and behavior change is inadequate.	• Reset priorities and redirect resources toward disease prevention and control.

Table 3.1 (*continued*) Menu of options for improving ICDS

Positive feature	Area needing improvement	How to do it
Care		
Designed to support effective nutrition counseling and growth promotion linked to regular growth monitoring.	*Anganwadi* workers are overburdened with tasks that take priority over promoting nutrition. *Anganwadi* workers receive little training to develop skills needed to counsel parents.	• Foster community support (for example, mothers groups). • Increase number of workers/helpers at *anganwadi* centers. • Improve training.
	Equipment and supplies for weighing and promoting growth are inadequate.	• Strengthen management information systems and improve the supply system.
	Emphasis on counseling and behavior change is inadequate.	• Reset priorities and redirect resources toward promoting appropriate breastfeeding, home-based complementary feeding, and caring behaviors. • Provide additional training.
Micronutrients		
Center-based interventions are potentially useful for supplementation of Vitamin A, iron, and folic acid.	Articulation with the Reproductive and Child Health Program is weak.	• Strengthen convergence with the Reproductive and Child Health Program.

Source: World Bank recommendations.

Improve Service Delivery at Existing Anganwadi *Centers*

Availability of funds has not been a major problem for ICDS, which has received extensive financing from both national and international sources. Over the years, both total spending and spending per child on various ICDS components has increased substantially (World Bank 2004d). The government of India's contribution increased from Rs329.8 *crores* in 1992/93 to Rs1,311.2 *crores* in 2001/02. Expenditure on supplementary nutrition, which is financed by state governments, increased by a factor of almost four during the same period.

Funding has increased, but it is not clear that the increase has had a measurable impact on children's nutritional status. Rather than expanding coverage, it might be more beneficial to allocate funds to improving service delivery at existing *anganwadi* centers.

Increase High-Level Commitment and Mobilize Political Leadership

High-level political commitment is key to all successful public health programs. India has one of the highest proportions of underweight children in the world, and the government has often expressed its commitment to reducing malnutrition. That commitment is not adequately reflected in current policy discussions, however.

Several factors may explain this. They include lack of awareness of the most cost-effective interventions, a tendency to view malnutrition interventions as transfers to the poor and to underestimate their economic impact on the country as a whole, the multiplicity of organizational stakeholders involved, and the relatively muted voice of the poor. To build commitment and mobilize political leadership toward supporting changes in the existing array of nutrition programs in India, public and private stakeholders will have to be made aware of the size and characteristics of the undernutrition problem in India; the devastating human, social, and economic consequences of failing to address the problem; and the substantial human, social, and economic benefits associated with the implementation of available, affordable, and cost-effective nutrition interventions.

Fix the Mismatches between Program Design and Implementation

ICDS has not yet effectively implemented the most cost-effective nutrition interventions or reached priority groups. Substantial changes in program implementation need to be introduced to fix the three most important mismatches.

Fix Mismatch I: Bridge the Gap between Program Design and Implementation so that the Most Important Causes of Undernutrition in India Are Addressed.

Feeding and caring practices. Although exclusive breastfeeding in the first months of life is important to avoid infection, water and other supplements are frequently given in early infancy (IIPS and Orc Macro 2000). A 2003 study in 49 districts revealed that only 40 percent of infants were exclusively breastfed during the first six months (BPNI 2003). Other studies indicate that the quality of complementary foods can be poor, due to local customs and beliefs (Roy 1997). Much needs to be done to reduce this source of nutritional deprivation during this crucial growth period.

The situation regarding the introduction of semi-solid complementary foods is even worse. According to the NFHS II (1998/99), only one-third of children in India were offered any semi-solid food between the ages of six and nine months. Along with infections, delayed introduction of semi-solid foods is an important trigger of malnutrition, which is worst between 6 months and 18–24 months. *Anganwadi* workers should devote much more attention to encouraging exclusive breastfeeding for the first six months and adding semi-solid complementary food three to four times a day in appropriate quantities thereafter (DWCD 2004b; Ghosh 2004).

Another key way to improve child growth is to show women how to use their own resources to feed their children more effectively. This approach has been used in many countries, including China, the Republic of Korea, and Vietnam (Whang 1981; Allen and Gillespie 2001). An intervention in Haiti taught mothers to use inexpensive local foods to prepare nutritious food for their children (King and others 1978; Berggren and others 1983; Scrimshaw 1995). The effort was highly successful in helping mothers rehabilitate their malnourished children: mortality rates of children whose mothers received demonstration-education were 68 percent of those of children whose mothers received growth-monitoring and counseling services but no demonstration-education. In households in which the mother participated in demonstration-education, the younger siblings of malnourished children were also less likely to become malnourished, and they had significantly lower mortality rates than the younger siblings of malnourished children whose mothers had not participated in demonstration-education. Similar positive effects of maternal knowledge and childcaring practices have been found in Bangladesh (Karim and others 2003). Promotion of feeding and caring practices is a critical aspect of ICDS that needs to be strengthened.

Disease control and prevention. Recognizing that child growth and health can be enhanced by improving environmental hygiene and domestic health management practices, the ICDS program includes components for deworming, iron supplementation for children, and home visits to improve childcare practices. Given the high prevalence of worm infestations and gastroenteric infections in India, these policies need to be implemented much more rigorously. *Anganwadi* workers need to be given more training and encouragement to implement these interventions and work with communities to improve their sanitary practices.

Collaboration between ICDS and the health delivery system has improved in recent years. One consequence of this collaboration has been better immunization coverage. The partnership between the *anganwadi* worker and the auxiliary nurse-midwife has been less successful with respect to identifying high-risk pregnancies, providing antenatal and postnatal care, and conveying adequate health and nutritional messages to women. Increased collaboration would help ensure the provision of broader child and maternal health services. Strengthening the convergence of ICDS and the Reproductive and Child Health Program should be a priority.

Micronutrient supplementation. ICDS can be used to facilitate children's access to national micronutrient supplementation programs for iron, Vitamin A, and iodine. These interventions have been shown to be exceptionally cost effective in a number of settings (Behrman, Alderman, and Hoddinott 2004), and their benefits for child growth, health, and cognitive development are well documented. To date, however, micronutrient interventions in India—namely, the distribution of iodized salt, the administration of a semi-annual massive dose of Vitamin A to young children, and the distribution of iron folic acid tablets to vulnerable groups—appear to have had little effect (Vijayaraghavan 2002). These programs need to be strengthened.

Supplementary feeding. ICDS functionaries at all administrative levels, as well as program beneficiaries, appear to consider the supplementary nutrition program (food distribution) to be synonymous with the full set of nutrition interventions of ICDS, often using the two concepts interchangeably. The confusion is indicative of the pervasiveness of the food bias in the ICDS program. The food bias is also evident in the allocation of expenditure across ICDS components: the supplementary feeding program accounts for about two-thirds of the total cost of the ICDS program (Radhakrishna, Ravi, and Indrakant 1998). It is important to use supplementary feeding strategically—as an incentive for poor and malnourished children to attend *anganwadi* centers, where they, and their mothers, can receive health and nutrition education interventions. It is crucial that ICDS implementation emphasize the multidimensional nature of malnutrition; that food intake be understood as only one, and most often not the main, determinant of child nutritional status; and that resources be redirected toward improving the delivery of other ICDS services.

Fix Mismatch II: Increase Impact by Reaching the Youngest Children. Because of the types of services provided and the focus on center-based activities, ICDS tends to reach mainly 3- to 6-year-olds, somewhat at the expense of pregnant women and children under 3. Young children need to be accompanied to the *anganwadi* center, and they require more time and attention than older children. Because fewer young children attend the center, interventions often miss this critical group. As a result, the prevalence of stunting and underweight remains very high.[35]

Failure to reach young children is of particular concern in light of the evidence that most growth faltering occurs during the first two years of life and that it negatively affects children's development throughout their lives (Allen and Gillespie 2001). A more concerted effort needs to be made to recruit young children into the program, perhaps by effectively reaching out to women while they are pregnant or just after they give birth. Recruiting more young children would produce a shift toward preventing malnutrition rather than treating it, often after it is too late to recover the growth trajectory. The advantage of some of the cost-effective measures described in table 3.1 is that unlike food supplementation, they are occasional interventions that do not require regular attendance at the *anganwadi* center (some can even be delivered in beneficiaries' homes). They are thus effective in reaching children under 3.

In this context, conditional cash transfers have been very successful in increasing the demand for health care for young children, educating parents about adequate caring and feeding practices, and rapidly improving child nutritional and health status in Colombia (Attansio, Syed, and Vera-Hernandez 2004), Honduras (Rawlings and Rubio 2003), and Mexico (Skoufias 2001). The possibility of introducing such programs in India should be explored.

Fix Mismatch III: Improve Targeting by Increasing Coverage in Poorer States and Districts. Another source of poor targeting lies in the regressive distribution of the ICDS program across states. The poorest states tend to receive the lowest government budgetary allocations per malnourished child. Thus the states with the highest prevalence of stunting and underweight tend to have the weakest program coverage.

There are some encouraging signs, though. First, the poorest states experienced the highest rate of growth of program coverage during the 1990s. Second, the program is more evenly distributed within states than across states: about 60 percent of the poorest villages in every state are covered by ICDS programs, compared with 70 percent of the wealthiest villages. Controlling for other village characteristics, within a given state, program placement is progressive.

The government of India has an action plan to construct another 188,000 *anganwadi* centers over the next few years. Given the high degree of concentration of child malnutrition in India, any future investment in ICDS should be driven by careful targeting of high-prevalence districts, villages, and settlements across the country. Unfortunately, available data cannot yet shed light on which villages should be chosen, because the sample surveys are not large or representative enough at the village level. However, promising new methodologies, based on the merging of household survey and census data, can help identify villages that are likely to have the highest prevalence of malnutrition. Targeting resources at villages based on their need is desirable not only for equity reasons—it is also the most effective strategy to reduce the prevalence of malnutrition.[36]

Improve Management on Site

Effective service delivery requires that trained and motivated workers are in place and have the supplies, equipment, transportation, and supervision to do their jobs well. This requires both adequate funding and good management. In some instances, strong management can partially compensate for budgetary restrictions.

A large number of studies document the implementation difficulties ICDS has experienced (NIPCCD 1992; Greiner and Pyle 2000; NCAER 2001; Allen and Gillespie 2001; Educational Research Unit 2004; Bredenkamp and Akin 2004). Some of these problems are due to the rapid expansion of the program, which has been faster than the institutional capacity necessary to manage it (World Bank 1998). Rapid expansion has not allowed *anganwadi* workers to be trained adequately. As a result, many workers have been sent to their centers with little or no training and have had to learn on the job. Refresher training is scarce, and adequate supervision is lacking. ICDS support services at the state level are inadequately staffed. As a result, although their job requires an understanding of nutrition, preschool education, and maternal and child health issues, *anganwadi* workers have very little technical or other support in providing ICDS services. Moreover, *anganwadi* workers are charged with a multiplicity of tasks, not all of them related to the central ICDS objectives. These responsibilities force them to divert some of their energies from the most important interventions. It is imperative that *anganwadi* workers be perceived and treated as the core input for ICDS service delivery and given the right tools and support to perform their tasks effectively.

A second problem is the erratic supply of food in ICDS. The national evaluation conducted in 1992 (NIPCCD 1992) found that the average *anganwadi* center was without food 20 percent of the time, and more than one-fourth of all centers experienced shortages that lasted longer than 3 months. Widespread delays in food distribution persist today (see table 2.3). Leakages in the distribution of ICDS food are substantial at many levels, notably in the procurement of food supplies (Greiner and Pyle 2000). In the absence of localized food insecurity (such as drought or crop failure), local procurement may be a more effective means of supplying food. Local procurement would probably increase the regularity of the food supply, since it is easier to hold local providers accountable for delivery, and local inhabitants would have a vested interest in the well-being of the children in their community. Moreover, local procurement provides a source of income to local inhabitants and promotes community awareness of and involvement in ICDS activities.

A third problem is the lack of growth-monitoring equipment. Many *anganwadi* centers do not have weighing scales that are in working condition, lack growth charts, or have insufficient numbers of growth cards. The monitoring and evaluation system fails to remedy shortfalls in supply.

Growth-monitoring activities are used to educate and encourage mothers to adopt behaviors that promote the growth of their children. It is in this area that the ICDS program is most lacking. It is critical that *anganwadi* workers be trained to conduct growth-monitoring and growth-promotion activities.

Use Information Effectively

Information can improve the effectiveness of ICDS in three ways. First, information about the extent of a problem raises awareness and focuses political and technical attention on finding solutions. Second, research on health behaviors and the effectiveness of different service delivery approaches can help shape the design of a program and increase its prospects for success. Third, information creates accountability and motivates.

It is generally recognized that monitoring and evaluation activities related to ICDS need strengthening, and a concerted effort is currently being made to do so. Toward this end, the Department of Women and Child Development might consider applying the monitoring and evaluation framework it uses for World Bank–funded ICDS projects to all ICDS projects.

High-quality information needs to be collected that is relevant, in the sense that the data clearly reveal something about the functioning of important aspects of the program. The quantity of data collected must be manageable, since large volumes of information are unlikely to be used to inform decisions. In this regard, it may be helpful to revisit the guidelines and instructions issued for the monitoring and evaluation of ICDS and to streamline and fine-tune them in an effort to reduce the volume of superfluous information and the time needed to process it. The number of registers currently collected by *anganwadi* workers, for example, far exceeds the capacity to use this information for program management.

Simultaneous with an effort to streamline and standardize the indicators collected across states should be the development of a standard template with which to display information. Such a template would make ICDS data more accessible at more levels and to more people in the project management system. Standardization would also facilitate comparisons across states, highlighting the states from which lessons can be learned in key areas of implementation. It would also promote the analysis of trends within states and the aggregation of data at the national level.

Computerization and electronic processing of information would greatly facilitate monitoring and evaluation. The challenge is to find a way of processing the data into a form that is usable, so that a program manager or other interested party can determine the status of activities—the percentage of a target group receiving benefits, the percentage of centers with weighing scales, whether food was received the previous month—at any point in time, past or present. Ideally, users should have easy access not only to aggregate indicators, but also to block- and district-level information. Periodically, quality control checks on monitoring data should be undertaken to uncover any systematic errors in reporting and identify the sources of any discrepancies. These changes would help transform the data collected by *anganwadi* centers into information that can be used to identify problems and to take the action needed to resolve them.

More human resources need to be devoted to monitoring and evaluation. One way to do so would be to increase awareness of the importance of monitoring at all levels of implementation, so that functionaries give these activities the attention they deserve. Creating awareness is challenging and requires a substantial mind shift for functionaries toward outcomes, results, and performance rather than inputs.

Strengthening of community monitoring is also desirable, through existing community institutions or, more informally, by encouraging community members to be alert to *anganwadi* center opening hours and attendance and demand improvements where needed.

Increase Decentralization and Community Participation

With few exceptions, ICDS remains a highly standardized intervention that follows rules and regulations set centrally. Given the heterogeneity of malnutrition patterns in India, state governments should be encouraged to tailor the basic model to local needs and assume responsibility for managing the overall program rather than focusing almost exclusively on the procurement and distribution of supplementary food (the only activity in the program they finance directly). A budget line that is specific to the financing of ICDS should be introduced in state budgets, so that the planning and monitoring of investments in ICDS becomes an explicit state-level activity.

ICDS is run in a very top-down fashion, with all the logistical and implementation inefficiencies and rigidities that such an approach entails. A program to provide daily services to young children and pregnant women requires strong participation and supervision by the community. There appears to be some empirical association between the strength of community support for ICDS, in the form of financial contributions from the *panchayat*, and the performance of *anganwadi* centers (Bredenkamp and Akin 2004). However, countrywide, only about 25 percent of states receive support from *panchayat* leaders, and this support has been mainly in the form of providing space for the *anganwadi* center and recruiting beneficiaries (NCAER 2001).

Despite statements of intent to involve communities in the process, there is little sense of community ownership (Greiner and Pyle 2000). This impression is reinforced by the fact that in most communities the *anganwadi* worker is hired and paid by the government and is not accountable to the community in which he or she works. Equipment, food, and other supplies are provided directly by the government. Because of their daily presence in the village, *anganwadi* workers are asked to take on many additional duties to support the field outreach staff of other government agencies (education, health, and rural development, in particular); they are not encouraged to work closely with community organizations, such as the *gram panchayat* or *mahila mandal*. Given the extensive decentralization that has been under way in India over the past decade, there is considerable scope for involving locally elected village committees much more actively in implementing ICDS. The experience of the mothers committees in Andhra Pradesh (see chapter 2) could be replicated in other states.

One important way to enhance the responsiveness of the ICDS program and cultivate a sense of local ownership is to always select the *anganwadi* worker from the community in which he or she works. Although included as a recommendation in the Department of Women and Child Development's guidelines, this does not always occur in practice: appointments are sometimes political or compassionate (made to people in difficult circumstances); sometimes they are even for sale. In many cases, the *anganwadi* worker is from a forward caste, which may affect the access of children from scheduled castes or tribes since, by their own admission, some *anganwadi* workers from forward castes make only infrequent home visits to scheduled caste hamlets (Educational Resource Unit 2004).

Next Steps: Rationalizing Design and Improving Implementation

ICDS has enormous potential to improve the nutritional status of India's children, but it needs to meet some challenges if this potential is to be realized. One challenge is the large and ever-increasing range of duties that *anganwadi* workers are expected to fulfill. Since, unlike most government workers, their workplace is located at the grass roots, they are asked to help implement a multiplicity of government programs in addition to ICDS. This diverts attention away from their core duties, which are already onerous and rarely can be performed satisfactorily. A second challenge is the fact that the changing scope of the ICDS has resulted in considerable ambiguity among higher-level officials as to the program's objectives, and the capacity of both the central and state units to manage and deliver the program is being stretched. A third challenge is the need to address the mismatches between what an effective nutrition intervention should do and what ICDS is currently doing.

Failure to meet these challenges is preventing ICDS from doing as much as it could to reduce the prevalence of malnutrition. It may be time to consider a new approach.

One option would be to retain the present structure, in which a preschool function for older children (4–6 years), on the one hand, and maternal and child health and nutrition interventions with special emphasis on younger children (0–3 years), on the other, are offered within the same program. If this option is pursued, the difficulties in simultaneously carrying out these disparate tasks need to be resolved. Under the current program, *anganwadi* workers devote most of their time to preschool education and older children, squeezing out attendance by younger children. Since *anganwadi* workers spend most of their remaining time preparing food, they have little time for health interventions or counseling parents about feeding and caring practices. If the present structure is maintained, introducing a system of two workers—one charged with health and nutrition functions, the other charged with the preschool function—may make sense. The National Rural Health Mission launched in fiscal 2005–6 plans to introduce an additional village health worker to focus on maternal and neonatal health issues. Such a worker could attend to the needs of children under 3, including nutrition. The *anganwadi* worker could focus on preschool education for older children and continue to prepare food. Coordination with the auxiliary nurse-midwife of the Reproductive and Child Health Program also needs to be carefully studied, defined, and monitored.

A more radical alternative would be to separate services provided to children 4–6 from those provided to younger children and pregnant and lactating women. The demand for preschool education and for feeding older children could be met by devolving these responsibilities to the Department of Education or to local authorities. The District Primary Education Program already delivers preschool education services in some districts; the feeding of children 4–6 could become part of the National Mid-Day Meals Program (Measham and Chatterjee 1999). In this manner, more of the *anganwadi* worker's time could be freed up for nutrition and health education and for growth promotion, increasing the prospect of achieving better nutrition outcomes. Coordination between the *anganwadi* worker, the auxiliary nurse-midwife, and the accredited social health activists (in the event that the proposal by the National Health Mission is implemented) will be crucial to the success of this effort.

Bridging the gap between the policy intentions of ICDS and its actual implementation probably represents the single greatest challenge in international nutrition. Meeting this challenge would have an enormous long-term impact on human development and economic growth.

Greater clarity and focus are needed if ICDS is to make a substantial dent in India's persistent undernutrition. In particular, the three mismatches identified in this report need to be resolved. Only by doing so can the program address the most important determinants of malnutrition, reach younger children and the most vulnerable segments of the population, and target areas in which the prevalence of undernutrition is highest. Leadership and commitment are required to address some of the structural inefficiencies of ICDS, including weak information systems, limited orientation toward results, and a lack of accountability for performance at all levels, that are hindering the program from achieving greater results.

Appendix

Table A.1 Responsiveness of prevalence of underweight to rising per capita GDP, 2002–15

Year	GDP per capita (billions)	Prevalence of underweight among children under 5 (percent)
2002	487.0	47.0
2003	501.6	46.3
2004	516.7	45.6
2005	532.2	44.9
2006	548.1	44.2
2007	564.6	43.5
2008	581.5	42.9
2009	599.0	42.2
2010	616.9	41.6
2011	635.4	40.9
2012	654.5	40.3
2013	674.1	39.7
2014	694.4	39.1
2015	715.2	38.5

Source: World Bank calculations.
Note: Calculations assume annual economic growth of 3 percent, exogenous income elasticity of malnutrition of 0.51, and percentage change in the prevalence of malnutrition of 2 percent.

Figure A.1 Weight-for-age estimates of change in nutritional status, in selected regions

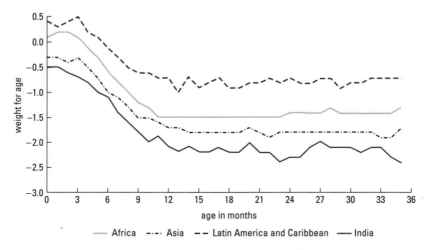

Source: Regional estimates from Shrimpton and others 2001; India data from IIPS and Orc Macro (2000).

Table A.2 Prevalence of anemia among children and women in India, by state, 1998–9 (*percent*)

State	Children under 3				Ever-married women 15–49			
	Mild	Moderate	Severe	Total	Mild	Moderate	Severe	Total
Andhra Pradesh	23.0	44.9	4.4	72.3	32.5	14.9	2.4	49.8
Arunachal Pradesh	29.1	24.7	0.7	54.5	50.6	11.3	0.6	62.5
Assam	31.0	32.2	0.0	63.2	43.2	25.6	0.9	69.7
Bihar	26.9	50.3	4.1	81.3	42.9	19.0	1.5	63.4
Delhi	22.2	42.9	3.9	69.0	29.6	9.6	1.3	40.5
Goa	23.5	27.9	2.0	53.4	27.3	8.1	1.0	36.4
Gujarat	24.2	43.7	6.7	74.5	29.5	14.4	2.5	46.3
Haryana	18.0	58.8	7.1	83.9	30.9	14.5	1.6	47.0
Himachal Pradesh	28.7	39.0	2.2	69.9	31.4	8.4	0.7	40.5
Jammu and Kashmir	29.1	38.5	3.5	71.1	39.3	17.6	1.9	58.7
Karnataka	19.6	43.3	7.6	70.6	26.7	13.4	2.3	42.4
Kerala	24.4	18.9	0.5	43.9	19.5	2.7	0.5	22.7
Madhya Pradesh	22.0	48.1	4.9	75.0	37.6	15.6	1.0	54.3
Maharashtra	24.1	47.4	4.4	76.0	31.5	14.1	2.9	48.5
Manipur	22.6	21.7	0.9	45.2	21.7	6.3	0.8	28.9
Meghalaya	23.4	39.8	4.3	67.6	33.4	27.5	2.4	63.3
Mizoram	32.2	22.7	2.3	57.2	35.2	12.1	0.7	48.0
Nagaland	22.0	18.7	3.0	43.7	27.8	9.6	1.0	38.4
Orissa	26.2	43.2	2.9	72.3	45.1	16.4	1.6	63.0
Punjab	17.4	56.7	5.9	80.0	28.4	12.3	0.7	41.4
Rajasthan	20.1	52.7	9.5	82.3	32.3	14.1	2.1	48.5
Sikkim	28.4	40.7	7.5	76.5	37.3	21.4	2.4	61.1
Tamil Nadu	21.9	40.2	6.9	69.0	36.7	15.9	3.9	56.5
Uttar Pradesh	19.4	47.8	6.7	73.9	33.5	13.7	1.5	48.7
West Bengal	26.9	46.3	5.2	78.3	45.3	15.9	1.5	62.7
India	22.9	45.9	5.4	74.3	35.0	14.8	1.9	51.7

Source: IIPS and Orc Macro 2000.

Table A.3 Percentage of villages covered by ICDS, by state, 1992/93–98/99

State	1992/93	1998/99
Andhra Pradesh	30	65
Arunachal Pradesh	65	82
Assam	39	30
Bihar	14	32
Delhi	53	55
Goa	85	95
Gujarat	61	84
Haryana	64	92
Himachal Pradesh	39	52
Jammu	44	70
Karnataka	63	86
Kerala	100	97
Madhya Pradesh	27	53
Maharashtra	66	81
Manipur	60	83
Meghalaya	07	22
Mizoram	97	73
Nagaland	54	84
Orissa	42	47
Punjab	39	70
Rajasthan	36	52
Sikkim	—	27
Tamil Nadu	77	43
Tripura	76	83
Uttar Pradesh	20	33
West Bengal	45	58
Total	35	52

Source: Calculated from NFHS (1992/93) and NFHS (1998/99) data by Lokshin and others (2005).
— Not available.

Figure A.2 Percentage of children attending *anganwadi* centers on daily basis, by age and state

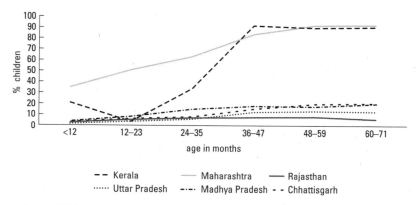

Source: ICDS III baseline/ICDS II endline survey 2000–2.

Table A.4 Percentage of children attending anganwadi centers, in villages with centers

Item	Kerala More than once a month	Kerala Daily	Maharashtra More than once a month	Maharashtra Daily	Rajasthan More than once a month	Rajasthan Daily	Uttar Pradesh More than once a month	Uttar Pradesh Daily	Madhya Pradesh More than once a month	Madhya Pradesh Daily	Chhattisgarh More than once a month	Chhattisgarh Daily
Total	54	49	75	62	10	6	24	6	35	12	47	10
Quintile												
Quintile 1 (poorest)	52	47	79	63	11	6	a	a	31	9	49	6
Quintile 2	53	48	77	60	10	7	24	6	34	10	48	9
Quintile 3	52	48	75	62	9	4	28	6	36	11	52	10
Quintile 4	54	49	73	69	11	5	25	7	34	11	47	11
Quintile 5 (richest)	56	51	66	52	11	6	18	4	40	24	41	13
Age												
3 and under	30	22	67	50	10	6	22	3	30	8	46	5
4–6	91	91	94	90	14	7	29	12	42	19	49	18
Gender												
Boys	54	49	75	62	10	5	24	6	34	12	47	10
Girls	53	48	75	62	11	6	24	6	36	12	48	10
Caste												
Scheduled caste	55	50	74	64	15	9	30	6	36	13	47	8
Scheduled tribe	49	45	79	65	11	7	19	4	41	14	50	11
Other backward groups	54	49	76	58	8	4	22	5	31	11	46	9
Other castes	53	48	71	60	9	5	20	6	34	15	44	11
Locality												
Urban	51	48	72	64	12	7	16	3	54	37	50	21
Rural	58	51	75	62	9	4	26	6	29	7	44	5
Tribal	45	39	79	60	11	7	—	—	43	15	51	10

Source: ICDS III Baseline/CDS II endline survey 2000–2.
— Not available.
a. Too few observations.

Table A.5 Receipt of health interventions during pregnancy under Care India's Integrated Nutrition and Health Project II (*percent*)

Intervention	All		Low SES		High SES	
	Intervention areas	Nonintervention areas	Intervention areas	Nonintervention areas	Intervention areas	Nonintervention areas
Consumption of 90+IFA	60	41*	62	40*	58	43
Tetanus toxoid (2+)	87	74*	91	70*	84	78
Antenatal checkups (3+)	53	38*	54	29*	53	53
Number of observations	189	151	69	83	120	68

Source: Personal communication with Care India.

* Statistically significant differences between intervention and nonintervention areas. IFA = iron and folic acid supplement.

Table A.6 Adoption of appropriate infant feeding behaviors under Care India's Nutrition and Health Project II (*percent*)

Feeding behaviour	All Intervention areas	All Nonintervention areas	Low socioeconomic status Intervention areas	Low socioeconomic status Nonintervention areas	High socioeconomic status Intervention areas	High socioeconomic status Nonintervention areas
Initiation of breastfeeding within 1 hour of birth	65.2 n=181	38.3* n=149	75.4 n=65	42.0* n=81	59.5 n=116	33.8* n=68
Exclusive breastfeeding for at least 6 months	69.3 n=189	57.6* n=151	69.6 n=69	63.9 n=83	69.2 n=120	50.0* n=68
Complementary feeding initiated (among 6- to 9-month-olds)	65.3 n=121	43.6* n=110	66.1 n=55	36.5* n=52	63.6 n=66	50 n=58
Among those who initiated complementary feeding, dietary diversity in complementary feeding						
vegetables given	68.0 n=203	43.6* n=156	62.9 n=89	50.7 n=75	71.9 n=114	37.0* n=81
oil added to food	41.9	20.5*	38.2	22.7*	44.7	18.5*
dal or animal foods given	79.8	55.8*	73.0	58.7	85.1	53.1*
Appropriate quantity, frequency, and diversity in feeding for age	6.1 n=244	0.5* n=218	2.8 n=106	0 n=109	8.7 n=138	0.9* n=109
Measles immunization by 12 months	55.4 n=121	35.1* n=111	47.3 n=55	25.0* n=52	62.1 n=66	44.1 n=59
Vitamin A (one dose) among children 9–11 months	59.5 n=121	43.2* n=111	49.1 n=55	44.2* n=52	68.2 n=66	42.4* n=59

Source: Personal communication with Care India.
* Statistically significant differences between intervention and nonintervention areas.

Notes

Chapter 1

1. The term *malnutrition* refers to both under- and overnutrition. India does have a small but increasing percentage of overweight children who are at risk for noncommunicable diseases such as diabetes and cardiovascular heart disease later in life. However, in view of the size and urgency of the undernutrition problem in India and its links to human development, this analysis deals only with undernutrition.

2. Clinical Vitamin A deficiency is a severe form of Vitamin A deficiency, which may result in xerophthalmia, a condition caused by inadequate functioning of the glands that produce tears. Symptoms include night blindness, Bitot's spots, xerosis, and keratomalacia. If not treated early enough, xerophthalmia can eventually lead to blindness. Subclinical Vitamin A deficiency is associated with increased vulnerability to a variety of infectious diseases and, therefore, an increased risk of mortality and morbidity.

3. Protein-energy malnutrition develops in children and adults whose consumption of protein and energy is insufficient. In most cases, both protein and energy deficiencies occur simultaneously. If protein deficiencies predominate, protein-energy malnutrition may manifest as kwashiorkor, which usually appears around the age of 12 months when breastfeeding ceases, but can also occur later in childhood. Kwashiorkor is characterized by edema, hair discoloration, and peeling skin. If energy deficiencies predominate, protein-energy malnutrition may manifest as marasmus, which usually develops in children 6–12 months who have been weaned from breastmilk or suffer from weakening infections, such as diarrhea. It is characterized by stunted growth and wasting.

4. Estimating the economic costs of malnutrition typically takes into account the prevalence of a particular macro- or micronutrient deficiency among men and women and their average levels of participation in market economic activity and heavy labor. Economic calculations are based only on market activities; they exclude non-market losses, even though they may be socially valuable. The calculations also require estimating the degree to which different nutritional conditions may coexist.

5. This estimate represents an upper bound, since the economic status of the child, for example, is unlikely to be completely independent of urban-rural location or caste.

6. Measuring the incidence of low birth weight in developing countries is challenging because of measurement error (as suggested by the heaping of data at the low birth weight cut-off of 2,500 grams) and because relatively few babies are weighed at birth.

7. The rural population of Delhi is not strictly comparable to the rural populations of other states, however, as most of Delhi's "rural" population consists of poor urban populations on the periphery of the city.

8. Principal component analysis, conducted on a set of variables including household assets and housing characteristics, was used to generate the cut-off points for the wealth tertiles, which divide the population of each state into three categories based on the individual's position in the India wealth distribution. Tertiles are used rather than quintiles because in some states there are too few observations available in some quintiles.

9. In the source data (DWCD and UNICEF 2001), reports of day and night-time vision problems were used as indicators of Vitamin A deficiency. However, it is likely that not all vision problems are Vitamin A–related and that there may be some under-reporting in disadvantaged areas due to poorer availability of diagnostic services.

10. Using 1990–2 data from rural areas, as well as the NFHS I (1992/93) and NFHS II (1998/99) data, Wagstaff and Claeson (2004) obtain an average annual reduction of 3.9 percent. Using a constant rate of change and data from NFHS I and NFHS II, Chhabra and Rokx (2004) and World Bank (2004a) obtain similar estimates (1.7 percent and 1.9 percent, with the difference attributable to rounding).

11. The rate shown for 1990 is projected from the change observed between the NFHS surveys conducted in 1992/93 and 1998/99. This MDG target is calculated for children under 3 and therefore differs from the WHO target, which focuses on children under 5.

12. The World Bank (2004a) estimates that reaching the 2015 MDG target is feasible under the following combination of economic growth and policy interventions: a 0.3 percent increase in average years of female schooling, a 4 percent increase in per child government expenditure on nutrition programs, a 3 percent increase in per capita consumption expenditure, a 1 percentage point increase in the coverage of regular electricity supply, a 1.5 percentage point increase in the population coverage of professionally assisted deliveries, a 1 percentage point increase in village access to *pucca* (blacktop) roads, and a 2 percentage point decrease in the population with no access to toilets since 1998/99.

Chapter 2

13. Together these factors constitute the concept of "nutrition security," which is viewed as the outcome of good health, a healthy environment, and good caring practices, combined with household-level food security.

14. For evidence from Peru, see Alderman, Hentschel, and Sabates (2003). For evidence from Andhra Pradesh, see Alderman, Hentschel, and Sabates (2003) and Gordon and Dunleavy (2001).

15. The Woman and Child Development Project supports ICDS service delivery in 11 states (Bihar, Chhattisgarh, Jharkhand, Kerala, Madhya Pradesh, Maharashtra, Orissa, Rajasthan, Tamil Nadu, Uttaranchal, and Uttar Pradesh). It includes a component that supports training for ICDS officials across India.

16. Among children under 3, the prevalence of underweight was 29.2 percent where the program was in place and 32.3 percent where it was not. Among children 3–6, the prevalence of underweight was 25.3 percent where the program was in place and 30.2 percent where it was not.

17. The percentage of children who receive any of ICDS's many services is difficult to estimate. The percentage of beneficiaries of the Supplementary Nutrition Program, one of the main ICDS services, is used as an indicator of the number of ICDS beneficiaries because data on this service is more readily available than other data.

18. This public expenditure estimate combines government expenditure on ICDS with state allocations to ICDS. It excludes any expenditure on ICDS by local government institutions.

19. Unless otherwise stated, "attendance" refers to visiting the *anganwadi* center at least once a month, conditional on there being a center in the village. (For figures on children's attendance, see appendix table A.4.) Since the villages and blocks in which households are located were not sampled randomly, the absolute levels of participation cannot be generalized to the entire state but only to the sampled blocks. The differentials in access by subgroup are likely to be more representative.

20. For disaggregated attendance rates by state, subgroup, and frequency of attendance, see appendix table A.4.

21. *Anganwadi* centers are located an average of 100–200 meters away from beneficiary households, with an average travel time of 5–10 minutes (NCAER 2001).

22. Similar findings were obtained in a countrywide study (NCAER 2001), which showed that just 17 percent of centers had toilets.

23.   These include records for daily attendance, preschool education, supplies, the supplementary nutrition program, births, deaths, immunization, weight, pregnancy, health referral, a daily dairy, a monthly progress report, and a survey of households in the area covered by the center.

24.   In some states, performance is better. In Chhattisgarh, for example, 95 percent of *anganwadi* centers report being visited by an auxiliary nurse-midwife every month.

25.   Most of these registers contain information on the take-up of different ICDS services, but *anganwadi* workers are also frequently charged with collecting information for other government programs, such as old-age schemes.

26.   Key indicators include figures on personnel, operationalization of blocks and *anganwadi* centers, supply of supplementary nutrition, preschool education, births and deaths, and malnutrition status using the IAP (Gomez) classification.

27.   The government has issued clearer monitoring and evaluation guidelines to the states, held annual and periodic review meetings at the central level, provided small supplementary financial allocations to monitoring and evaluation activities at the local level, and plans to revise the monitoring formats and the number of *anganwadi* center registers. In World Bank project states, ICDS input, process, and impact indicators that are compatible with the project's development objectives were defined at the outset of the project, and adequate financial allocations were made to the monitoring and evaluation component of ICDS. Monitoring and evaluation activities include field visits, periodic reviews, operations research, continuous social assessments, and baseline and endline surveys, in addition to the standard ICDS monitoring activities.

28.   In Madhya Pradesh only 58 percent of urban *anganwadi* centers had been visited by supervisors in the previous month.

29.   In Chhattisgarh 43 percent of *anganwadi* workers were not linked to supervisors.

30.   This project is implemented in partnership with the Department of Women and Child Development and the Department of Health and Family Welfare of the Government of India, nongovernmental organizations, and community-based organizations, with support from USAID and its BASICS II project for child survival. It is being implemented in Andhra Pradesh, Bihar, Chhattisgarh, Jharkhand, Madhya Pradesh, Orissa, Rajasthan, Uttar Pradesh, and West Bengal.

31.   Interventions include antenatal care, nutrition counseling, and birth preparedness; home-based newborn care; maternal and child immunization; child feeding advice; vitamin A supplementation for children; and supplementary nutrition.

32.   This section draws on research by the International Food Policy Research Institute (IFPRI 2003).

33. The target number of committees is 53,144, which will cover all *anganwadi* centers in Andhra Pradesh.

Chapter 3

34. Technological innovation is not considered, because it is not likely to play a key role in this type of nutrition intervention.

35. Many of these problems were addressed in Tamil Nadu's modification of the ICDS program (TINP), which halved the prevalence of severe malnutrition in the villages in which it was implemented by targeting food to the needy and requiring them to eat it on the premises instead of taking it home to share with others (Heaver 2002; Greiner and Pyle 2000).

36. See World Bank (2004a) for an explanation of the concentration of child malnutrition and possible methodologies for improving targeting.

Bibliography

ACC/SCN (United Nations Administrative Committee on Coordination/Standing Committee on Nutrition). 1997. *Third Report on the World Nutrition Situation.* Geneva: ACC/SCN.

———. 2000. *Fourth Report on the World Nutrition Situation: Nutrition throughout the Life Cycle.* Geneva: ACC/SCN.

———. 2004. *Fifth Report on the World Nutrition Situation: Nutrition for Improved Development Outcomes.* Geneva: ACC/SCN.

Adhikari, S. 2004. "Monitoring and Evaluation in India's ICDS Programme." Background paper for this report.

Agarwal, D.K., K.N. Agarwal, K. Satya, and S. Agarwal. 1998. "Weight Gain During Pregnancy: A Key Factor in Perinatal and Infant Mortality." *Indian Pediatrics* 35 (8): 733–44.

Agarwal, S., A. Agarwal, A.K. Bansal, D.K. Agarwal, and K.N. Agarwal. 2002. "Birth Weight Patterns in Rural Undernourished Pregnant Women." *Indian Pediatrics* 39 (3): 244–53.

Alderman, H. 2005. "Linkages between Poverty Reduction Strategies and Child Nutrition: An Asian Perspective." *Economic and Political Weekly* 40 (46): 4837–42.

Alderman, H., J. Hentschel, and R. Sabates. 2003. "With the Help of One's Neighbors: Externalities in the Production of Nutrition in Peru." *Social Science and Medicine* 56 (10): 2019–31.

Alderman, H., J. Behrman, V. Lavy, and R. Menon. 2001. "Child Health and School Enrollment: A Longitudinal Analysis." *Journal of Human Resources* 36 (1): 185–205.

Allen, H.E., D.W.T. Crompton, N. De Silva, P. T. Loverde, and G.R. Olds. 2002. "New Policies for Using Antihelmintics in High-Risk Groups. *Trends in Parasitology* 18: 381–82.

Allen, L.H. 1994. "Nutritional Influences on Linear Growth: A General Review." *European Journal of Clinical Nutrition* 48, Suppl. 1: S75–S89.

Allen, L.H., and S.R. Gillespie. 2001. *What Works? A Review of the Efficacy and Effectiveness of Nutrition Interventions.* Manila: Asian Development Bank, in collaboration with ACC/SCN.

Anand, K., S. Kant, and S.K. Kapoor. 1999. "Nutritional Status of Adolescent School Children in Rural North India." *Indian Pediatrics* 36 (8): 810–16.

ASC (Administrative Staff College of India). 1998. *National Strategy to Reduce Child Malnutrition.* Hyderabad.

Attanasio, O., M. Syed, and M. Vera-Hernandez. 2004. "Early Evaluation of a New Nutrition and Education Programme in Colombia." Briefing Note No. 44. Institute for Fiscal Studies, London.

Barker, D.J.P., T. Forsèn, A. Uutela, C. Osmond, and J.G. Eriksson. 2001. "Size at Birth and Resilience to Effects of Poor Living Conditions in Adult Life: Longitudinal Study." *British Medical Journal* 323 (7324): 1273–76.

Beaton, G., R. Martorell, and K. Aronson. 1993. *Effectiveness of Intermittent Iron Supplementation in the Control of Iron Deficiency Anemia in Developing Countries: An Analysis of Experience.* Final Report to the Micronutrient Initiative, Ottawa.

Behrman, J.R., H. Alderman, and J. Hoddinott. 2004. "Copenhagen Consensus: Challenges and Opportunities: Hunger and Malnutrition." *Copenhagen Consensus Challenge Papers.* May 7.

Bentley, M.E., and P.L. Griffiths. 2003. "The Burden of Anemia among Women in India." *European Journal of Clinical Nutrition* 57 (1): 52–60.

Berggren G., W. Berggren, A. Verly, N. Gamier, and W. Peterson. 1983. "Traditional Midwives, Tetanus Immunization, and Infant Mortality in Rural Haiti." *Tropical Doctor* 13 (2): 79–87.

Bhandari, L., and L. Zaidi. 2004. "Reviewing the Costs of Malnutrition in India." Background paper for this report.

Black, M.M. 2003. "Micronutrients Deficiencies and Cognitive Functioning." *Journal of Nutrition* 133 (11): S3927–31.

Black, R.E., S.S. Morris, and J. Bryce. 2003. "Where and Why Are 10 Million Children Dying Every Year?" *Lancet* 361 (9376): 2226–34.

Bleichrodt, N., and M.P. Born. 1994. "A Meta-Analysis of Research on Iodine and its Relationship to Cognitive Development." In *The Damaged Brain of Iodine Deficiency: Cognitive, Behavioral, Servomotor and Educative Aspects,* ed. J.B. Stanbury, 279–85. New York: Cognizant Communication Corporation.

Bouis, H., and J. Hunt. 1999. "Linking Food and Nutrition Security: Past Lessons and Future Opportunities." *Asian Development Review* 17 (1, 2): 168–213.

BPNI (Breastfeeding Promotion Network of India). 2003. *Status of Infant and Young Child Feeding in 49 Districts, 98 Blocks.* New Delhi: BPNI.

Bredenkamp, C., and J.S. Akin. 2004. "India's Integrated Child Development Services Scheme: Meeting the Health and Nutritional Needs of Children, Adolescent Girls and Women?" Background paper for this report.

Calder, P.C., and A.A. Jackson. 2000. "Undernutrition, Infection and Immune Function." *Nutritional Research Reviews* 13 (1): 3–29.

Care India. 2004. *Implementing an Integrated Package of Nutrition and Health Interventions. Lessons from the Early Learning Phase of INHP II, May 2002 to August 2003.* New Delhi.

Care India and Linkages India. 2003. *Profiles for India 2003.* New Delhi: Care India.

Caulfied, L., M. De Onis, M. Blössner, and R.E. Black. 2004. "Under-Nutrition as an Underlying Cause of Child Deaths Associated with Diarrhea, Pneumonia, Malaria, and Measles." *American Journal of Clinical Nutrition* 80 (1): 193–98.

Census of India. 2001. *Basic Population Data.* http://www.censusindia.net/t_00_005.html.

Chhabra, R., and C. Rokx. 2004. "The Nutrition MDG Indicator: Interpreting Progress." HNP Discussion Paper, World Bank, Washington, DC.

Collins, W.J., and M.A. Thomasson. 2002. "Exploring the Racial Gap in Infant Mortality Rates, 1920–1970." Working Paper No. 02–W01, Vanderbilt University, Department of Economics, Nashville, TN.

Daniels, M., and L. Adair. 2004. "Growth in Young Filipino Children Predicts Schooling Trajectories through High School." *Journal of Nutrition* 134 (6): 1439–46.

De Onis, M., M. Blössner, E. Borghi, E.A. Frongillom, and R. Morris. 2004. "Estimates of Global Prevalence of Childhood Underweight in 1990 and 2015." *Journal of the American Medical Association* 291 (21): 2600–06.

Dev, S. Mahendra. 2004. "Analysis of Public Expenditures and Impact of Public Distribution System (PDS) on Food Security." Background paper for this report.

DWCD (Department of Women and Child Development). 2003. *The Indian Child: A Profile.* http://wcd.nic.in/indianchild/index.htm.

———. 2004a. *UDISHA.* http://wcd.nic.in/udisha/htm/services.htm.

————. 2004b. *National Guidelines on Infant and Young Child Feeding*. Department of Women and Child Development, New Delhi.

————. 2005. *Annual Report 2004–2005*. New Delhi: Department of Women and Child Development.

DWCD (Department of Women and Child Development), and UNICEF. 2001. *Multiple Indicator Survey 2000 (MICS–2000): India Summary Report*. November. Department of Women and Child Development, New Delhi.

Educational Resource Unit. 2004. "Analysis of Positive Deviance in the ICDS Program in Rajasthan and Uttar Pradesh." Background paper for this report.

Esrey, S.A., J.B. Potash, L. Roberts, and C. Shiff. 1990. *Health Benefits from Improvements in Water Supply and Sanitation: Survey and Analysis of the Literature on Selected Diseases*. WASH Technical Report 66, Water and Sanitation for Health Project, Arlington, VA.

Fawzi, W.W., T.C. Chalmers, and M.G. Herrera. 1993. "Vitamin A Supplementation and Child Mortality: A Meta-Analysis." *Journal of the American Medical Association* 269 (7): 898–903.

Ghosh, S. 2004. "Child Malnutrition." *Economic and Political Weekly* 39 (40): 4412–14.

Glewwe, P., H. Jacoby, and E. King. 2001. "Early Childhood Nutrition and Academic Achievement: A Longitudinal Analysis." *Journal of Public Economics* 81 (3): 345–68.

Gopalan, C. 1981. *The National Goitre Control Programme: A Sad Story*. Nutrition Foundation of India, New Delhi. http://nutritionfoundationofindia.res.in/archives.asp?archiveid=35&back=byauthor.asp.

————. 1992. "Growth Charts in Primary Child-Health Care: Time for Reassessment." *Indian Journal of Maternal and Child Health* 3 (4): 98–103.

Gordon, J.E., M.A. Guzman, W. Ascoli, and N.S. Scrimshaw. 1964. "Acute Diarrhoeal Disease in Less Developed Countries: Patterns of Epidemiological Behaviour in Rural Guatemalan Villages." *Bulletin of the World Health Organization* 31: 9–20.

Gordon, K.L., and M. Dunleavy. 2001. *Environmental Health in India: Priorities in Andhra Pradesh*. World Bank, South Asia Region, Environment and Social Development Unit, Washington, DC.

Grantham-Mcgregor, S.M., and C.C. Ani. 2001. "Undernutrition and Mental Development." In *Nestlé Nutrition Workshop Series Clinical and Performance Program 5*, ed. J.D. Fernstrom, R. Uauy, and P. Arroyo, 1–18. Basel: Nestlé Ltd.

Greiner, T., and D.F. Pyle. 2000. India: Nutrition Assessment. World Bank, Washington, DC.

Haddad, L., H. Alderman, S. Appleton, L. Song, and Y. Yohanes. 2003. "Reducing Malnutrition: How Far Does Income Growth Take Us?" *World Bank Economic Review* 17 (1): 107–13.

Heaver, R. 2002. "India's Tamil Nadu Nutrition Program: Lessons and Issues in Management and Capacity." HNP Discussion Paper. World Bank, Washington, DC.

Heston, A., R. Summers, and B. Aten. 2002. *Penn World Tables Version 6.1.* University of Pennsylvania, Center for International Comparisons, Philadelphia.

Horton, S. 1999. "Opportunities for Investments in Nutrition in Low-Income Asia." *Asian Development Review* 17 (1, 2): 246–73

Horton, S., and J. Ross. 2003. "The Economics of Iron Deficiency." *Food Policy* 28 (1): 51–75.

Horton, S., T. Sanghvi, M. Philipps, J. Fiedler, R. Perez-Escamilla, C. Lutter, A. Rivera, and A.M. Segall-Correa. 1996. "Breastfeeding Promotion and Priority Setting in Health." *Health Policy and Planning* 11 (2): 156–58.

Hunt, J.M. 2004. "Costs of Halving Global Hunger: Reducing Micronutrient Deficiencies and Child Underweight Prevalence in Accord with the Millennium Development Goals #1 and #4." Background paper prepared under management of the International Food Policy Research Institute for the United Nations Hunger Task Force.

IFPRI (International Food Policy Research Institute). 2003. *New and Noteworthy in Nutrition* 40. Washington, DC.

IIPS (International Institute for Population Sciences). 1995. *National Family Health Survey (NFHS –1), 1992–93, India.* Mumbai.

IIPS (International Institute for Population Sciences), and Orc Macro. 2000. *National Family Health Survey (NFHS–2), 1998–99, India.* Mumbai.

Johri, N. 2004. *Effect of Integrated Program Design on Child Health Inputs and Outcomes: Estimates from a Nutrition and Health Program in India.* PhD dissertation, University of North Carolina, Department of Health Policy and Administration, Chapel Hill.

Jones, G., R.W. Steketee, R.E. Black, Z.A. Bhutta, S.S. Morris, and the Bellagio Child Survival Study Group. 2003. "How Many Child Deaths Can We Prevent this Year?" *Lancet* 362 (9377): 65–71.

Jonsson, U. 1993. "Integrating Political and Economic Factors within Nutrition-Related Policy Research: An Economic Perspective." In *The Political Economy of Food and Nutrition Policies*, ed. P. Pinstrup-Andersen, 193–205. Baltimore, MD: Johns Hopkins University Press.

Kapil, U., P. Pathak, M. Tandon, C. Singh, R. Pradhan, and S.N. Dwivedi. 1999. "Micronutrient Deficiency Disorders amongst Women in Three Urban Slum Communities of Delhi." *Indian Pediatrics* 36 (10): 983–89.

Karim, R,, S.A. Lamstein, M. Akhtaruzzaman, K.M. Rahman, and N. Alam. 2003. *The Bangladesh Integrated Nutrition Project: Endline Evaluation of the Community-Based Nutrition Component.* Institute of Nutrition and Food Science, University of Dhaka, Dhaka.

King, K.W., W. Fougere, A. Hilaire, R.E. Webb, W. Berggren, and G. Berggren. 1978. "Preventive and Therapeutic Benefits in Relation to Cost: Performance over Ten Years of Mothercraft Centers in Haiti." *American Journal of Clinical Nutrition* 31 (4): 679–90.

Kulkarni, M.N., and Y.N. Patthabi. 1988. "Evaluation of the Effectiveness of ICDS in 7 Anganwadi Centres on the Health Status of Pre-School Children." *Indian Journal of Community Medicine* 13 (2): 86–90.

Levine, R., and the What Works Working Group. 2004. *Millions Saved: Proven Successes in Global Health.* Center for Global Development, Washington, DC.

Lokshin, M., M. Das Gupta, M. Gragnolati, and O. Ivaschenko. 2005. "Improving Child Nutrition: The Integrated Child Development Services in India." *Development and Change* 36 (4): 613–40.

Lucas, A., M.S. Fewtrell, and T.J. Cole. 1999. "Fetal Origins of Adult Disease: The Hypothesis Revisited." *British Medical Journal* 319 (7204): 245–49.

Macintyre, C.R., N. Kendig, L. Kummer, S. Birago, and N.M. Graham. 1997. "Impact of Tuberculosis Control Measures and Crowding on the Incidence of Tuberculous Infection in Maryland Prisons." *Clinical Infectious Diseases* 24 (6): 1060–67.

Martorell, R., J.P. Habicht, C. Yarbrough, A. Lechtig, R.E. Klein, and K.A. Western. 1975. "Acute Morbidity and Physical Growth in Rural Guatemalan Children." *American Journal of Diseases in Children* 129 (11): 1296–1301.

Mason, J.B., P. Musgrove, and J.P. Habicht. 2003. "At Least One-Third of Poor Countries' Disease Burden Is Due to Malnutrition." Working Paper 1, National Institutes of Health, Fogarty International Center, Disease Control Priorities Project, Bethesda, MD.

Mason, J., A. Bailes, M. Beda-Andourou, N. Copeland, T. Curtis, M. Deitchle, L. Foster, M. Hensley, P. Horjus, C. Johnson, T. Lloren, A. Mendez, M. Munoz, J. Rivers, and G. Vance. 2005. "Recent Trends in Malnutrition in Developing Regions: Vitamin A Deficiency, Anemia, Iodine Deficiency, and Child Underweight." *Food and Nutrition Bulletin* 26 (1): 59–108.

Mata, L.J., R.A. Kromal, J.J. Urrutia, and B. Garcia. 1977. "Effect of Infection on Food Intake and the Nutritional State: Perspectives as Viewed from the Village." *American Journal of Clinical Nutrition* 30 (8): 1215–27.

Measham, A.R., and M. Chatterjee. 1999. *Wasting Away: The Crisis of Malnutrition in India.* Washington, DC: World Bank.

Ministry of Agriculture. 2002. *Agricultural Statistics at a Glance 2003.* Government of India, New Delhi.

Ministry of Industry. 2000. *Sustaining Elimination of Iodine Deficiency Disorders: Universal Salt Iodization in India. Historical Overview and Future Strategies.* Government of India, New Delhi.

Mkenda, A.F. 2004. "The Benefits of Malnutrition Interventions: Empirical Evidence and Lessons from Tanzania." Unpublished manuscript.

Moe, C.L., M.D. Sobsey, G.P. Samsa, and V. Mesolo. 1991. "Bacterial Indicators of Risk of Diarrhoeal Disease from Drinking Water in the Philippines." *Bulletin of the World Health Organization* 69 (3): 305–17.

Murray, C.J.L., and A.D. Lopez. 1997. "Global Mortality, Disability and the Contribution of Risk Factors: Global Burden of Disease Study." *Lancet* 349 (9063): 1436–42.

NCAER (National Council of Applied Economic Research). 2001. *Concurrent Evaluation of Integrated Child Development Services.* New Delhi.

New Concept Information Systems. 2004. "Literature Review of MDM, ICDS, and PDS (1992–2003), Including Annotated Bibliography." Background paper for this report.

NFHS (National Family Health Survey) II database. Mumbai: International Institute for Population Sciences (IIPS).

NIPCCD (National Institute of Public Cooperation and Child Development). 1992. *National Evaluation of Integrated Child Development Services.* New Delhi.

NNMB (National Nutrition Monitoring Bureau). 2002. *Diet and Nutritional Status of Rural Population.* Hyderabad: NNMB.

NSS (National Sample Survey Organisation). 1997. *NSS 53rd Round 1997.* New Delhi.

———. 2001. *NSS 56th Round 2000–2001.* New Delhi.

———. 2002. *NSS 57th Round 2001–2002.* New Delhi.

Nutrition Foundation of India. 1991. *Growth Performance of Affluent Indian Children.* Scientific Report No. 11. New Delhi.

Orc Macro. 2004. *Measure DHS Statcompiler.* http://www.measuredhs.com/statcompiler/ start.cfm?action=new_table&userid=170232&usertabid=186282&CFID=659299& CFTOKEN=41841064.

Pandav, C.S., K. Anand, S. Gupta, and G.V. Murthy. 1998. "Cost of Vitamin A and Iron Supplementation to 'At Risk' Population." *Indian Journal of Pediatrics* 65 (6): 849–56.

Pelletier, D.L., and E.A. Frongillo. 2003. "Changes in Child Survival Are Strongly Associated with Changes in Malnutrition in Developing Countries." *Journal of Nutrition* 113 (1): 107–19.

Pelletier, D.L., E.A. Frongillo, Jr., and J.P. Habicht. 1993. "Epidemiologic Evidence for a Potentiating Effect of Malnutrition on Child Mortality." *American Journal of Public Health* 83 (8): 1130–33.

Pelletier, D.L., E.A. Frongillo, D.G. Schroeder, and J.P. Habicht. 1995. "The Effects of Malnutrition on Child Mortality in Developing Countries." *Bulletin of the World Health Organization* 73 (4): 443–48.

Planning Commission. 2003. *Annual Report 2002–2003.* Government of India, New Delhi.

Popkin, B.M., S. Horton, S.W. Kim, A. Mahal, and J. Shuigao. 2001. "Trends in Diet, Nutritional Status, and Diet-Related Non-Communicable Diseases in China and India: The Economic Costs of the Nutrition Transition." *Nutrition Reviews* 59 (12): 379–90.

Radhakrishna, R., C. Ravi, and S. Indrakant. 1998. *Cost Effectiveness and Efficiency of the Nutrition Programmes in India.* Center for Economics and Social Studies, Hyderabad.

Ramalingaswami V., U. Jonson, and J. Rohde. 1997. "The Asian Enigma." In *The Progress of Nations.* New York: UNICEF.

Ramaswami, B. 2002. "Efficiency and Equity of Food Market Interventions." *Economic and Political Weekly* 37 (12): 1129–35.

Rawlings, L., and G. Rubio. 2003. "Evaluating the Potential of Conditional Cash Transfer Programs." *World Bank Research Observer* 20 (1): 29–55.

Ross, J., and S. Horton. 1998. *Economic Consequences of Iron Deficiency.* Micronutrient Initiative, Ottawa.

Ross, J.S., and E.L. Thomas. 1996. *Iron Deficiency Anemia and Maternal Mortality.* Profiles 3, Working Notes Series No. 3. Academy for Education Development, Washington, DC.

Roy, S.K. 1997. "Complementary Feeding in South Asia." In *Malnutrition in South Asia: A Regional Profile*, ed. S. Gillespie, 51–73. Kathmandu: UNICEF Regional Office for South Asia.

Saiyed, F. and A. Srivastava. 2005. "Project Dular (Love) Goes to More Children in Jharkhand." *UNICEF India*. http://www.unicef.org/india/health_963.htm.

Schürch, B., and N.S. Scrimshaw. 1989. *Activity, Energy Expenditure and Energy Requirements of Infants and Children*. Proceedings of an International Dietary Energy Consultancy Group Workshop held in Cambridge, MA, November 14–17.

Scrimshaw, N.S., ed. 1995. *Community-Based Longitudinal Nutrition and Health Studies: Classical Examples from Guatemala, Haiti and Mexico*. Boston: International Nutrition Foundation for Developing Countries.

Scrimshaw, N.S. and J.P. SanGiovanni. 1997. "Synergism of Nutrition, Infection, and Immunity." *American Journal of Clinical Nutrition* 66 (2): 464S–77S.

Scrimshaw, N.S., M.A. Guzmán, M. Flore, and J.E. Gordon. 1968. "Nutrition and Infection Field Study in Guatemalan Villages, 1959–1964: V. Disease Incidence among Preschool Children under Natural Village Conditions, with Improved Diet and Medical and Public Health Services." *Archives of Environmental Health* 16: 223–34.

Seshadri, S. 2001. "Prevalence of Micronutrient Deficiency Particularly of Iron, Zinc and Folic Acid in Pregnant Women in South East Asia." *British Journal of Nutrition* 85, Suppl. 2: S87–S92.

Sethi, D., P. Cumberland, M.J. Hudson, L.C. Rodrigues, J.G. Wheeler, J.A.Roberts, D.S. Tompkins, J.M. Cowden, and P.J. Roderick. 2001. "A Study of Infectious Intestinal Disease in England: Risk Factors Associated with Group A Rotavirus in Children." *Epidemiology and Infection* 126 (1): 63–70.

Shekar, M., M. de Onis, M., M. Blössner, and E. Borghi. 2004. "Will Asia Meet the Nutrition Millennium Development Goal? And Even if it Does, Will it Be Enough?" Background paper for this report.

Shrimpton, R., C.G. Victora, M. De Onis, R.C. Lima, M. Blossner, and G. Clugston. 2001. "Worldwide Timing of Growth Faltering: Implications for Nutritional Interventions." *Pediatrics* 107 (5): E75.

SIDA (Swedish International Development Cooperation Agency). 2000. *Reaching Out to Children in Poverty: The Integrated Child Development Services in Tamil Nadu, India*. Department of Democracy and Social Development, Stockholm.

Singh, P., and G.S. Toteja. 2003. "Micronutrient Profile of Indian Children and Women: Summary of Available Data for Iron and Vitamin A." *Indian Pediatrics* 40 (5): 477–99

Skoufias, E. 2001. *Progresa and its Impacts on the Human Capital and Welfare of Households in Rural Mexico: A Synthesis of the Results of an Evaluation by IFPRI*. International Food Policy Research Institute, Washington, DC.

Smith, L., and L. Haddad. 2000. *Explaining Child Malnutrition in Developing Countries: A Cross-Country Analysis*. Research Report 111, International Food Policy Research Institute, Washington, DC.

Stephensen, C.B. 2003. "Vitamin A, (Beta)-Carotene, and Mother-to-Child Transmission of HIV." *Nutrition Reviews* 61 (8): 280–84.

Subramaniyam, P. 2004. "Case Study on Mid-Day Meal Scheme of Tamil Nadu and Gujarat." Background paper for this report.

UNICEF (United Nations Children's Fund). 1990. Strategy for Improved Nutrition of Children and Women in Developing Countries. *UNICEF Policy Review* 1990–1 (E/Icef/1990/L.6). New York: UNICEF.

———. 1998. *The State of the World's Children 1998: Focus on Nutrition*. New York: Oxford University Press.

———. 2003a. *The State of the World's Children. 2003*. New York: UNICEF.

———. 2003b. *UNICEF Statistics: Malnutrition*. New York: UNICEF.

———. 2004. *A Glance: India*. http://www.unicef.org/infobycountry/india.html.

UNICEF (United Nations Children's Fund) and MI (Micronutrient Initiative). 2004a. *Vitamin and Mineral Deficiency: A Global Damage Assessment Report*. http://www.micronutrient.org/resources/publications.asp.

———. 2004b. *Vitamin and Mineral Deficiency: A Global Progress Report*.

Vasundhara, M.K., and B.N. Harish. 1993. "Nutrition and Health Education through ICDS." *Indian Journal of Maternal and Child Health* 4 (1): 25–26.

Vijayaraghavan, K. 2002. "Control of Micronutrient Deficiencies in India: Obstacles and Strategies." *Nutrition Reviews* 60 (5) Suppl.1: 73–76.

Vijayaraghavan, K., and H.D. Rao. 1998. "Diet and Nutrition Situation in Rural India." *Indian Journal of Medical Research* 108: 243–45.

Vinutha, B., M.N. Mehta, and P. Shanbag. 2000. "Vitamin A Status of Pregnant Women and Effect of Post-Partum Vitamin A Supplementation." *Indian Pediatrics* 37 (11): 1188–93.

Wagstaff, A., and M. Claeson. 2004. *Rising to the Challenges: The Millennium Development Goals for Health*. Washington, DC: World Bank.

West, K.P. 2002. "Extent of Vitamin D Deficiency among Preschool Children and Women of Reproductive Age." *Journal of Nutrition* 132 (9): 2857s–66s.

Whang, I. 1981. *Management of Rural Change in Korea*. Seoul: Seoul National University Press.

WHO (World Health Organization). 1995. *Physical Status: The Use and Interpretation of Anthropometry*. Report of a WHO Expert Committee. WHO Technical Report Series 854, Geneva.

———. 2000. *Nutrition Profile of the WHO: South-East Asia Region*. Regional Office for South-East Asia, New Delhi.

———. 2002. *World Health Report 2002: Reducing Risks, Promoting Healthy Life*. Geneva.

———. 2004a. *Global Database on Iodine Deficiency Disorders: India*. Geneva.

———. 2004b. *Micronutrient Deficiency. Battling Iron Deficiency Anaemia: The Challenge*. Geneva.

———. 2004c. *WHO Global Database on Child Growth and Malnutrition*. Geneva.

World Bank. 1998. *Implementation Completion Report on the Second Tamil Nadu Integrated Nutrition Project*. Operations Evaluation Department. Washington, DC.

———. 2003. *Mid-Term Survey for the Andhra Pradesh Economic Restructuring Project (APERP)-Nutrition/ICDS Component*. Washington, DC.

———. 2004a. *Attaining the Millennium Development Goals in India: How Likely and What Will It Take to Reduce Infant Mortality, Child Malnutrition, Gender Disparities and Hunger-Poverty and to Increase School Enrollment and Completion*. Washington, DC.

———. 2004b. *Global Development Finance 2004: Harnessing Cyclical Gains for Development*. Washington, DC.

———. 2004c. *India Burden of Disease Statistics*. Washington, DC.

———. 2004d. *Reaching Out to the Child. An Integrated Approach to Child Development*. New Delhi: World Bank

———. 2004e. *World Development Indicators 2004*. Washington, DC.

Index

ECO-AUDIT
ENVIRONMENTAL BENEFITS STATEMENT

The World Bank is committed to preserving endangered forests and natural resources. We have chosen to print *India's Undernourished Children: A Call for Reform and Action* on recycled paper with 30 percent post-consumer fiber. The World Bank has formally agreed to follow the recommended standards for paper usage set by the Green Press Initiative, a non-profit program supporting publishers in using fiber that is not sourced from endangered forests. For more information, visit www.greenpressinitiative.org.

The printing of these books on recycled paper saved the following:

- 8 trees (40' in height, 6–8 inches in diameter)

- 371 pounds of solid waste

- 2,888 gallons of water

- 696 pounds of net greenhouse gases

- 6 million BTUs of total energy